1

The Shoes of the Jews: Enduring Trials

Garry Glaub

ISBN #: 978-0-9847533-3-8

Cover Photo taken by Garry Glaub in Glamis, California, at the Imperial Sand Dunes. Back cover taken by Garry Glaub in Glamis, California, in the Imperial Sand Dunes.

Please enjoy other books written by Garry Glaub:
"Here Am I! Send Me." (A Commentary on Isaiah 1-23)
To God Be the Glory Daily Devotional
Throughout Your Generations, a Christian Seder
Strength & Beauty, the Book of Ruth

Table of Contents:

Dedication:

⁶ In this you greatly rejoice, though now for a little while, if need be, you have been grieved by various trials, ⁷ that the genuineness of your faith, being much more precious than gold that perishes, though it is tested by fire, may be found to praise, honor, and glory at the revelation of Jesus Christ, ⁸ whom having not seen you love. Though now you do not see Him, yet believing, you rejoice with joy inexpressible and full of glory, ⁹ receiving the end of your faith—the salvation of your souls.
1 Peter 1:6-9 (NKJV)

How awful it would be to walk this world alone. Those of us who now walk with the LORD remember what it was like before our lives changed. There are atheists who seem to have all they could ever ask for, but happiness still eludes them. As death approaches for all of us, no amount of money can stave off death. How sad it would be if the fleeting moments of pleasure we find on this earth were everything. Instead, we know that trials will come, but we have a future and a hope. This book is dedicated to the One who gives that future, for my hope is in Him!

Preface:

Life has more ups and downs than a day at Disneyland, but though all of us should be accustomed to those changes, we seem to forget that at the end of each valley is another mountain. Even when we know that the mountaintop experience is just a little more of a climb, we tend to complain with each step of difficulty. As Christians, most of us can look back at our past to find that moment of brokenness when we finally stopped looking for a solution other than the obvious one of Jesus Christ. Though brokenness brought us to Him, we still hesitate to welcome more brokenness in our lives. Sadly, we also tend to doubt God when faced with hardship, though He has promised to never leave us or forsake us. Instead of remembering God's saving grace and merciful hand of support in all aspects of our lives, we often can wallow in self-pity with an attitude of "what are You going to do for me now, God?"

It is a difficult decision when beginning a book about enduring trials. For when we pray that the LORD teach us valuable lessons about any aspect of life, He is more than likely to comply, being that He did promise us that the Holy Spirit will teach us all things! If we pray for patience, we soon find ourselves in situations that call for us to exhibit that patience. Similarly, if we want to learn how to endure trials, we certainly will find a bumpy rode ahead in life's journey. One of the greatest admonitions of prayer is to be careful what we ask for. Though we can hesitate to ask for trials, the most important part of that trial is the outcome. God's desire is to draw us closer to Him. Consequently, that end result of closeness with Him is worth any cost.

God uses trials in our lives in a variety of ways, and often, accomplishes many parts of His plan simultaneously. While that increased closeness with Him in our personal relationships often can be the most important aspect of a trial, we also can gain much-needed compassion along the way, as well. Compassion has been described as feeling someone else's pain. This is much easier from memory than it is from imagination. For example, it is very difficult for a man to envision the pain of a woman in labor, but a woman who has given birth to children easily can remember what that was like! In a similar manner, God often places us in situations where we can exhibit our compassion. Notice how many former drug addicts become involved in substance-abuse ministries. That must be one of the reasons that God chose to send His Son to redeem us. Jesus took the form of a man, and while on this earth, felt every pain, every temptation and every challenge that each of us feel. We cannot make excuses to God of "You don't know what it's like!" Being omniscient, He does know what it is like, and Jesus demonstrated that He could endure it all without sinning. Sadly, we cannot last a day without sinning!

One of the greatest aspects of enduring a trial is to remember how often we fail. That failure can involve falling away from God, but as Christians, we always can see that God will use our greatest failures and worst decisions for our good and for His glory. This demonstratres Romans 8:28 in a close and personal way. When we look back on our own failures, it is much easier to show compassion as well as grace when we are confronted by companions on the same journey who also have failed.

Contentment in all things seems to be a very important goal. Paul was a great example of a man whose contentment had nothing to do with earthly prosperity or physical well-being. A Christian who exhibits joy in the midst of great difficulty is a proverbial megaphone to a deaf world. Sometimes, that joy can help convince an unbeliever that Jesus is the answer.

So let us begin this journey on enduring trials. In the midst, develop a sensitivity to others who are sharing the same road. But most importantly, realize that our goal is a closer walk with Jesus!

If you have questions or comments, feel free to email me at:
gg4jesus@gmail.com
or visit my website at:
www.garryglaub.com

Chapter 1,
Trials, Temptations &
Tribulation

Before studying what the Bible has to say about enduring trials, we need to understand what a trial really is. Most Christians have heard the words test, trial, temptation and tribulation bandied about, but few grasp the sometimes-subtle nuances that separate these words and corresponding circumstances from each other. Likely the first step in enduring a trial is being able to identify that trial! Let's begin with a study of the usage of the word trial in the Bible. Interestingly, the word for trial and temptation is the same Hebrew word, *masah*,

מסה

In the New Testament, trial and temptation also share the same Greek word, *peirasmos*.

πειρασμός .

Though the words are the same, they are used in different contexts. Think of the word 'appealing' in English. One usage of 'appealing' may apply to a man who has been convicted in a trial and would like another trial, while a different usage of 'appealing' may apply that same man's description of a woman he is interested in. Though both use the same word, it is simple for us to understand and identify which is occurring in a sentence. With 'trial' and 'temptation,' if the Greek and Hebrew words are the same in both cases, there should be stark similarities. While every temptation is a trial of our faith, it appears that every trial is a temptation for us to give in to sin. The differences between trial and temptation are numerous. While trials come from God, temptations always come from the flesh, though we can group Satan and his demons into that group of tempters. Satan has been around a long time, and has instructed his demons to tempt everyone. Through temptation, Satan appeals to our sin nature, desiring for us to choose momentary pleasure over God's moral code. Even Jesus, immediately after His baptism, went into the wilderness where Satan tempted Him for 40 days. Temptation seems to take the same form as it did for Eve in the Garden of Eden; Jesus in the wilderness; and for each of us as well, as it seems like Satan has found a strategy he prefers:

16 For all that is in the world—the lust of the flesh, the lust of the eyes, and the pride of life—is not of the Father but is of the world. 17 And the world is passing away, and the lust of it; but he who does the will of God abides forever.
1 John 2:16-17 (NKJV)

Each of these temptations falls into one of those three categories: the lust of the flesh, the lust of the eyes and the pride of life. Eve's flesh lusted for the taste of the fruit; in the wilderness, Jesus fasted for 40 days and His flesh certainly hungered. So Satan attempted to coerce Jesus into turning the rocks into bread; for us, Satan and his demons appeal to our fleshly desires for food, alcohol, sex, etc. In addition to the lust of the flesh, Eve also failed in regard to the lust of the eyes. The fruit coming from the tree of knowledge of good and evil was beautiful. How that fruit tasted was no longer a concern. Eve wanted its beauty. Many years later in the wilderness, Satan tried the same ploy on Jesus, taking him to the highest point. Looking down to the beautiful cities below, Satan offered to elevate Jesus to be the ruler of those cities. Notice that Jesus did not comment upon Satan's inability to offer that status, for Jesus knew that God had granted Satan dominion over this earth, for a time. Once again, Satan wants us to desire beauty, but true beauty is not what is on the outside.

One night, a Christian man took his family to a mountain overlooking the plains, which were filled with cities and city lights. He asked his children what they thought about those lights. "They are absolutely beautiful," said the son. "Now, look up," the father instructed. Sitting on that mountain, the family admired the lights in the sky, the moon and the stars. "Those are the lights that God created," said the man, "and those are the lights that man created," pointing to the city lights. "Which are more beautiful?" The perceived beauty that Satan has created often gratifies our flesh. While God creates a beautiful body, Satan displays its nakedness and causes man's flesh to lust. Finally, let's look at the pride of life in the Garden of Eden:

⁴ Then the serpent said to the woman, "You will not surely die. ⁵ For God knows that in the day you eat of it your eyes will be opened, and you will be like God, knowing good and evil." Genesis 3:4-5 (NKJV)

Satan understands that pride of life! According to Isaiah 14, Lucifer was the ranking angel in heaven, but led a rebellion against God that included one-third of the angels. In the same passage, God tells us that Satan desired to be "like the Most High" God. In the wilderness, Satan brought Jesus to Jerusalem:

⁹ Then he brought Him to Jerusalem, set Him on the pinnacle of the temple, and said to Him, "If You are the Son of God, throw Yourself down from here. ¹⁰ For it is written: 'He shall

give His angels charge over you, To keep you,' [11] and, 'In their hands they shall bear you up, Lest you dash your foot against a stone.' " [12] And Jesus answered and said to him, "It has been said, 'You shall not tempt the LORD your God.'
Luke 4:9-12 (NKJV)

In His comment to Satan, Jesus quoted Deuteronomy 6:16, stating, "You shall not tempt the LORD your God." 'Tempt' is the same word for 'try,' a shortened version of 'trial.' Satan enticed Eve to sin through his temptation, and he entices each of us in the same deceitful manner. But Jesus demonstrated to us that with His strength, we are able to walk the same path and deny Satan's advances. Temptations coerce us to break God's Laws, while trials can be morally neutral, like a person becoming ill, losing their job or being passed over for a promotion at work.

Trials, simply stated, are difficult events we must endure because we continue to exist in a broken and sinful world. Once the LORD has completed His work in us and we are united with Him for eternity, both trials and temptations will cease to exist. If having difficulty deciphering which is occurring, look more closely at the cause. Trials come from God, while temptations come from Satan. Think of Job. God allowed the difficulties in Job's life for a definite purpose; that purpose was to draw Job closer to the LORD. In the midst of that trial, Satan also tempted Job, enticing him into a place of pride. Job denied his own sin and became accusative toward God. While the end result of temptation is either sin or denial of that sin, the end result of trial is a closer walk with Jesus. We grow through trials. If the principal of an elementary school schedules a fire drill every week, it has nothing to do with his attempt to burn the school to the ground. Instead, he desires for the children to learn and grow, so if and when a similar difficulty arises, the children will respond correctly. Enduring that annoying siren and the ensuing process is a trial in the lives of those children. We have heard the adage that what does not kill us makes us stronger, and God strengthens us under duress. He refines us in his fire of trials:

⁶ In this you greatly rejoice, though now for a little while, if need be, you have been grieved by various trials, ⁷ that the genuineness of your faith, being much more precious than gold that perishes, though it is tested by fire, may be found to praise, honor, and glory at the revelation of Jesus Christ, ⁸ whom having not seen you love. Though now you do not see Him, yet believing, you rejoice with joy inexpressible and full of glory, ⁹ receiving the end of your faith—the salvation of your souls.
1 Peter 1:6-9 (NKJV)

Trials reveal our faith and help it to grow! Temptation often can bring out our worst, but trials can bring out our best! It may not seem that way in all parts of the trial, but with God's helping hand, we usually feel that way when the trial is over. That being said, we can fail in the midst of trial, and sadly, if God has a certain result in mind, we may have to endure the same trial again if we have not learned the lesson He desired for us to learn. Most Christians pray for trials to cease, and this is fine, as long as we are praying in the same manner of "Thy kingdom come, Thy will be done, on earth as it is in heaven." For when we see our Savior face-to-face, those trials will end. Maybe we should be praying that we learn exactly what God desires for us the first time we endure a trial, so we do not have to go through the same trial again! Until we are with our LORD for eternity, trials will be tools that God uses to stretch us. Instead of complaining in the midst of trial, we should rejoice!

¹² Beloved, do not think it strange concerning the fiery trial which is to try you, as though some strange thing happened to you; ¹³ but rejoice to the extent that you partake of Christ's sufferings, that when His glory is revealed, you may also be glad with exceeding joy.
1 Peter 4:12-13 (NKJV)

Once again, let's understand once and for all that no one ever is

19

tempted by God:

**¹³ Let no one say when he is tempted, "I am tempted by God";
for God cannot be tempted by evil, nor does He Himself
tempt anyone. ¹⁴ But each one is tempted when he is drawn
away by his own desires and enticed. ¹⁵ Then, when desire has
conceived, it gives birth to sin; and sin, when it is full-grown,
brings forth death.**
James 1:13-15 (NKJV)

Certainly Satan has a part in all of our sins. We speak of the
original sin of Adam and Eve in the Garden, but Satan's fall from
grace came before Adam's fall. That angel of light has become the
great deceiver, who lies to coerce our sin, and then
approaches God as the accuser of the brethren, pointing out our
failures. Sadly, many of our sins begin in our own minds. Though
God has given us new hearts, we retain those old brains. If we
only would remember our past sin along with the brokenness it
caused. Instead, most of us remember the pleasure associated with
sin and choose to forget that brokenness. As Proverbs 26 reminds
us, a fool returns to sin just as a dog returns to lick up his own
vomit! If offended by the disgusting nature of this remark,
understand that our sin is much more disgusting than regurgitated
food!

Finally, we need to add the word 'tribulation' to this list. Jesus
said,

**These things I have spoken to you, that in Me you may have
peace. In the world you will have tribulation; but be of good
cheer, I have overcome the world."**
John 16:33 (NKJV)

Tribulation in the New Testament is the Greek word *thlipsis*,
θλίψις, and refers to pressing or pressure. For a Christian, this can
be anything that burdens the spirit. To understand tribulation,

reflect upon what Jesus endured. The people He came to save did not accept Him! He stood over Jerusalem and wept!

41 Now as He drew near, He saw the city and wept over it, 42 saying, "If you had known, even you, especially in this your day, the things that make for your peace! But now they are hidden from your eyes. 43 For days will come upon you when your enemies will build an embankment around you, surround you and close you in on every side, 44 and level you, and your children within you, to the ground; and they will not leave in you one stone upon another, because you did not know the time of your visitation."
Luke 19:41-44 (NKJV)

Tribulation also can refer to a woman in childbirth or a man in war. Both of those pains are great, but do not compare to the pain of a rejected Savior. Additionally, tribulation also refers to a 7-year period like no other in the world's existence, in which mankind receives the wrath of a rejected God. Never forget, even in His wrath, God loves perfectly, as He desires repentance, redemption and relationship for each of us.

Finally, let's put this together, before proceeding into numerous Bible studies concerning trials and enduring those trials. A springboard to understanding this concept is in Psalms:

8"Do not harden your hearts, as in the rebellion,
As in the day of trial in the wilderness,
9 When your fathers tested Me;
They tried Me, though they saw My work.
10 For forty years I was grieved with that generation,
And said, 'It is a people who go astray in their hearts,
And they do not know My ways.'
11 So I swore in My wrath,
'They shall not enter My rest.' "
Psalm 95:8-11 (NKJV)

This passage speaks of a specific rebellion that occurred during the exodus, the 40-year journey of the Jews from Egypt to the Promised Land. In verse 8, we see the word 'trial.' Remember, this is a lengthened version of the word 'try,' as in "try it, you'll like it." God does not mind if we try Him on for size, so to speak, before we make any commitment. What we will find is His size is immense, immeasurable and immutable! The Jews tested God and tried Him, according to verse 9, "though they saw" His work! His work included parting the Red Sea and vanquishing their enemies; included speaking to them from the holy mountain when He gave them His commandments; included a pillar of cloud by day and a pillar of fire by night that protected them and remained with them; included daily provision that fell from heaven each day in a food they called *manna*, though the Jews even made fun of His daily bread! Finally, God disallowed anyone over 20 from entering His Promised Land, not holding the children accountable for the sins and murmurings of their parents. What was "the day of trial in the wilderness?"

A clue lies in the Hebrew words of this passage. The Hebrew word for 'trial' is *masah*:

מסה

This word can mean trial, temptation, or the name of the place where the Jews tested Jehovah, Massah. At the same time, the word for 'rebellion' in verse 8 is *meribah*.

מריבה

Massah and Meribah? Sounds familiar!

¹ Then all the congregation of the children of Israel set out on their journey from the Wilderness of Sin, according to the commandment of the Lord, and camped in Rephidim; but there was no water for the people to drink. ² Therefore the people contended with Moses, and said, "Give us water, that we

may drink." So Moses said to them, "Why do you contend with me? Why do you tempt the Lord?"
³ And the people thirsted there for water, and the people complained against Moses, and said, "Why is it you have brought us up out of Egypt, to kill us and our children and our livestock with thirst?"
⁴ So Moses cried out to the Lord, saying, "What shall I do with this people? They are almost ready to stone me!"
⁵ And the Lord said to Moses, "Go on before the people, and take with you some of the elders of Israel. Also take in your hand your rod with which you struck the river, and go. ⁶ Behold, I will stand before you there on the rock in Horeb; and you shall strike the rock, and water will come out of it, that the people may drink." And Moses did so in the sight of the elders of Israel. ⁷ So he called the name of the place Massah and Meribah, because of the contention of the children of Israel, and because they tempted the Lord, saying, "Is the Lord among us or not?"
Exodus 17:1-7 (NKJV)

God instructed Moses to strike the rock to provide water for the complaining Jews. Lest we forget, the Jews were walking through the hot desert, and our complaints involve much less basic needs than water in the desert. Just as the Jews should have recognized His hand of protection and provision and not questioned God, we should also accept what He chooses to give as the perfect gift! Sadly, the Jews seemed to be right back in the same location years later:

¹ Then the children of Israel, the whole congregation, came into the Wilderness of Zin in the first month, and the people stayed in Kadesh; and Miriam died there and was buried there.
² Now there was no water for the congregation; so they gathered together against Moses and Aaron. ³ And the people contended with Moses and spoke, saying: "If only we had died when our brethren died before the Lord! ⁴ Why have you

23

brought up the assembly of the Lord into this wilderness, that we and our animals should die here? [5] And why have you made us come up out of Egypt, to bring us to this evil place? It is not a place of grain or figs or vines or pomegranates; nor is there any water to drink." [6] So Moses and Aaron went from the presence of the assembly to the door of the tabernacle of meeting, and they fell on their faces. And the glory of the Lord appeared to them.

[7] Then the Lord spoke to Moses, saying, [8] "Take the rod; you and your brother Aaron gather the congregation together. Speak to the rock before their eyes, and it will yield its water; thus you shall bring water for them out of the rock, and give drink to the congregation and their animals." [9] So Moses took the rod from before the Lord as He commanded him.

[10] And Moses and Aaron gathered the assembly together before the rock; and he said to them, "Hear now, you rebels! Must we bring water for you out of this rock?" [11] Then Moses lifted his hand and struck the rock twice with his rod; and water came out abundantly, and the congregation and their animals drank. [12] Then the Lord spoke to Moses and Aaron, "Because you did not believe Me, to hallow Me in the eyes of the children of Israel, therefore you shall not bring this assembly into the land which I have given them."

[13] This was the water of Meribah, because the children of Israel contended with the Lord, and He was hallowed among them.
Numbers 20:1-13 (NKJV)

This may seem like the same event, but a major difference occurs. When once again accosted by the complaints of thirst by his people, Moses went to the LORD. Instead of striking the rock, this time the LORD told Moses to speak to the rock. In anger, Moses once again struck the rock (twice), and just as before, the rock yielded enough water for all of the people and the livestock. Sadly, by striking the rock instead of speaking to it, Moses greatly angered the LORD, and because of this event, Moses was not allowed to enter the Promised Land. Why? That seems to be a minor difference, like the spirit of the law compared to the letter of the law. Does that not seem like a heavy punishment for a seemingly minor infraction?

Regardless of what we see, Moses disobeyed God. Yet when we understand this event prophetically, God's reaction makes more sense. The rock is a symbol of Jesus, who as our Chief Cornerstone, is the Rock of our salvation. When He came to save us, He died, and on that day at Calvary, Jesus was struck. When He returned to heaven, He never would be struck again. When He returns, He never will endure that kind of abuse again. But Moses struck the rock again! Yet even if God chose to punish Moses for what we see as a minor infraction, that is His choice, and He only makes those choices with all of the information in His hands!

Another interesting part of this biblical tale is that both events occurred in the same location. Remember, the Jews took 40 years to complete a journey that only would have taken 11 days if they traveled directly. Instead, their sin caused the wandering in the wilderness to continue. On their first visit there, God even named the site 'Temptation and Contention,' Massah and Meribah, after their complaints. Sadly, it does not appear that the Jews recognized this location when thirsty again. There seems to be no remembrance of the previous contention with God. Our lives also contain repetitious trials. God has the ability to take us to the woodshed as many times as He deems necessary for us to learn the lesson He desires!

At Massah and Meribah, the people tested God. They disobeyed and complained, to see how far He would allow them to go. Remember the comments of Jesus to Satan when asked to throw Himself from the top of the temple, quoting from Deuteronomy:

"You shall not tempt the Lord your God as you tempted Him in Massah.
Deuteronomy 6:16 (NKJV)

Again, 'tempt' and 'try' are the same word in Hebrew and the same word in Greek. Notice that Satan tempted God at Massah, not just the Jews! What does it mean to 'try' or 'tempt' God? Well, in the case of Jesus, Satan wanted Him to launch Himself from the Temple, knowing that God's angels would protect Him. If we feel that God will protect us no matter what, if we jump off the Empire State Building, God has the ability to save us if He desires, but He also has created the natural laws of gravity. After jumping, if we pray for His miraculous hand of salvation, the likely result would be a lot of our DNA splattered on the pavement below. God is still a God of miracles, and is wrapped intricately into every part of the lives of His children. He 'proves' Himself to us with His daily provision and protection, though we often take His gifts for granted.

Though God is slow to anger, the actions of His dumb sheep certainly can bring Him to the point of that anger. Jesus came to follow God's Law and live a sinless life. He was not about to 'tempt' God. When the Jews 'tempted' Him, He did not allow them to enter into the Promised Land. (Neither did Moses get to enter at that time, but we know he was there at the Mount of Transfiguration with Jesus)! Instead of us 'trying' God, He is 'trying' us!

²³ **Search me, O God, and know my heart;**
Try me, and know my anxieties;
²⁴ **And see if there is any wicked way in me,**
And lead me in the way everlasting.
Psalm 139:23-24 (NKJV)

God 'tries' us through trials, which are circumstances that can test a strength and expose a weakness. Each of those trials contains His handprint. Think of Abraham, whom God commanded to sacrifice his son, Isaac. In Genesis 22, we see that God did not require Abraham to perform that most difficult task, but before God released Abraham from that requirement, Abraham demonstrated his willingness to the LORD. Then God provided His own sacrifice in a male, unblemished ram. We also should test ourselves:

⁵ Examine yourselves as to whether you are in the faith. Test yourselves. Do you not know yourselves, that Jesus Christ is in you?—unless indeed you are disqualified. ⁶ But I trust that you will know that we are not disqualified.
2 Corinthians 13:5-6 (NKJV)

Once again, that test can reveal depth or a lack of depth. Any test has a measurement, and in the case of testing ourselves, we are measuring our lives against God's Laws, and the lives He has called for us to live. God tests us in trials continuously. If God is omniscient, what is the purpose of putting us into those situations, as He already knows how we will react? The purpose is not so He can see how we will react. Instead, God's purpose is so we can see that He shows up in the middle of every one of our trials! Just as He remained as the pillar of cloud and pillar of fire each day in the lives of the Jews, His chosen people, He dwells within us now. If we do not see God in the midst of our trials, it is because we have walked away from Him. All we need to do is turn around and look. He is there!

Blessed is the man who endures temptation; for when he has been approved, he will receive the crown of life which the Lord has promised to those who love Him.
James 1:12 (NKJV)

DISCUSSION QUESTIONS:

1. Can you give an example of a trial that you had to endure more than once before learning the intended lesson?

2. What was the most difficult trial you experienced as a Christian?
3. Give a biblical example, other than Abraham, of a trial that God called one of His followers to endure.
4. Are there any temptations that we must give in to?
5. In modern times, we can sometimes blame some of our sins of addiction on sickness, rather than choice. If we continue to give in to the same sin, can we ever conquer that sin? Why or why not?

Notes:

Notes:

Chapter 2,
The Shoes of the Jews

A wise person once uttered the words, "You can eat an elephant one bite at a time," referring to enduring any hardship by taking small steps. Some of our obstacles are nothing more than hurdles, taking only one step to cross and to place in the memory banks. Yet other obstacles seem to go on for years. Even those lasting difficulties are conquerable, thanks to the LORD's guidance. We may not have endurance alone, but God supernaturally can sustain us through anything! We sometimes place limits on what He is capable of doing, when God has no limits. He remains a God of miracles, and lest we forget, He made all of the laws of the universe. Our LORD can change those laws if He desires, just as He made the sun stand still! Remember that interesting passage in Joshua:

[12] **Then Joshua spoke to the Lord in the day when the Lord delivered up the Amorites before the children of Israel, and he said in the sight of Israel:**
"Sun, stand still over Gibeon;
And Moon, in the Valley of Aijalon."

¹³ So the sun stood still,
And the moon stopped,
Till the people had revenge
Upon their enemies.
Is this not written in the Book of Jasher? So the sun stood still
in the midst of heaven, and did not hasten to go down for about
a whole day. ¹⁴ And there has been no day like that, before it or
after it, that the Lord heeded the voice of a man; for the Lord
fought for Israel.
Joshua 10:12-14 (NKJV)

While God is capable of ostentatious miracles like the stopping of
the sun or the parting of the Red Sea, the seemingly smaller
miracles that He performs in our lives reveal how much He really
loves us, as He is intricately woven into every aspect of the life of
a believer. God knows the number of hairs on each of our heads!
He knows our thoughts before we think them. He knows exactly
how long our trials will last.

During the exodus, God parted the Red Sea and vanquished the
advancing Egyptian armies, the enemies of the children of Israel.
When His children complained of hunger, God fed them with
manna. When they were thirsty, Moses struck a rock with his staff
and they received water from God. Let's look at another miracle
that God accomplished for the Jews during their exodus:

⁵ "And I have led you forty years in the wilderness. Your
clothes have not worn out on you, and your sandals have not
worn out on your feet. ⁶ You have not eaten bread, nor have
you drunk wine or similar drink, that you may know that I am
the Lord your God.
Deuteronomy 29:5-6 (NKJV)

This book gets its title from this verse, though the verse is often
overlooked. Once again, this displays God's miraculous hand in
the lives of His childen, a common theme of the Bible. Doubtfully,

none of us own shoes worn daily with soles that have lasted four decades! We thought God was concerned with our souls, but it is evident that He also is concerned with our soles. It is likely that when God made this comment to the children of Israel about His performance of this miracle that none of the Jews even had noticed that a miracle had occurred! Sometimes, we are so wrapped up in our own complaints that we fail to notice God's miraculous provision. Instead, we should notice and thank Him for each gift. Sadly, God is well aware of our desperately wicked hearts, and those hearts contain a heaping dose of unthankfulness.

Notice that the verses in Deuteronomy do not point to God's claim of keeping their sandals and clothing in brand-new condition. It is difficult to think of any item that most of us would prefer to be slightly worn, rather than brand-spanking new more than shoes! How often do new shoes cause our feet to blister? Some well-worn items we are hesitant to throw away, like an old leather chair that fits every contour of our bodies. Shoes and sandals are similiar, as they are softer and more pliable. Additionally, our feet become calloused in places where those blisters have occurred in the past. A new or different pair of shoes frequently causes that cycle to begin anew.

Walking in sand might be less abrasive to the soles, but the rest of the sandal takes a greater amount of abuse than normal in desert terrain, as the path is not flat. Instead, desert travel contains an inordinate amount of ascending and descending, twisting and turning. Rarely do a pair of sandals endure one summer at the beach today!

In the same manner that God can make shoes endure the elements as well as our abuse, He can protect His children from wearing out! One of the most common catch-phrases of modern times is "burned out." The typical workweek used to last six days. It was not until 1908 that a New England cotton mill instituted a two-day weekend to enable Jews to observe their Sabbath on Saturdays, in addition to the Christian Sabbath of Sundays. Many workers have lengthened that to a three-day weekend, putting in a few extra hours via "flex time" on their four-day workweek. Interestingly, as the number of hours spent in labor seems to be decreasing, the number of people complaining of "burn-out" seems to be increasing.

As Christians, we should not "burn out," but instead, should have our lamps burning brightly for Him! Paul is a perfect example. With all that Paul endured, many would ascertain that his body was too broken to continue. In his own words, Paul tells us:

23 Are they ministers of Christ?—I speak as a fool—I am more: in labors more abundant, in stripes above measure, in prisons more frequently, in deaths often. 24 From the Jews five times I received forty stripes minus one. 25 Three times I was beaten with rods; once I was stoned; three times I was shipwrecked; a night and a day I have been in the deep; 26 in journeys often, in perils of waters, in perils of robbers, in perils of my own countrymen, in perils of the Gentiles, in perils in the city, in perils in the wilderness, in perils in the sea, in perils among false brethren; 27 in weariness and toil, in sleeplessness often, in hunger and thirst, in fastings often, in cold and nakedness— 28 besides the other things, what comes upon me daily: my deep concern for all the churches.
2 Corinthians 11:23-28 (NKJV)

In the verses above, Paul was not bragging about the abuse he had endured for his steadfast belief in the risen Savior. Instead, he was truthfully giving an accounting. He had studied under the most respected rabbi, Gamaliel, and had much intellectual knowledge concerning the Old Testament. He worked strongly against Christians and the spread of Christianity. Yet when confronted from the heavens by the risen Savior while on the road to Damascus, Paul's life changed on the spot (Acts 9). Forced to question the intellectual decisions of his life to that point, Paul devoted the remainder of his life to sharing the gospel of Jesus Christ with everyone in his path. He preached to Jews and Gentiles alike. Scholars believe the hunch-backed Paul was short, had a speech impediment and suffered from eye problems. Regardless of his physical limitations, Paul spoke with the Lord's power. What did Paul receive from his resolve to share the love of the Lord? Hardship, torture, shipwrecks and imprisonment. When we travel, we ask about the amenities of the nicest hotels. Paul asked about the jails!

Today, most of our pastors prepare a sermon each week, and some others might prepare two. Paul, on the other hand, worked as a tentmaker during the week. Instead of a congregation supporting Paul, he supported himself.

[1] After these things Paul departed from Athens and went to Corinth. [2] And he found a certain Jew named Aquila, born in Pontus, who had recently come from Italy with his wife Priscilla (because Claudius had commanded all the Jews to depart from Rome); and he came to them. [3] So, because he was of the same trade, he stayed with them and worked; for by occupation they were tentmakers. [4] And he reasoned in the synagogue every Sabbath, and persuaded both Jews and Greeks.
Acts 18:1-4 (NKJV)

Paul did not go on sabbatical for a year to recharge his batteries. Instead, he stayed busy in the LORD's service until he died, glad to serve his Savior. George Whitefield is worth studying, as well. An 18th-century, Anglican Protestant minister, Whitefield bridged the gap of Christian belief between those in pre-Revolution America, as Methodists, Baptists, Puritans, Quakers and followers of other religious denominations flocked to hear him preach. In 34 years of speaking God's truth, Whitefield preached over 18,000 sermons, an average of more than a sermon each day! Similar to Paul, Whitefield did not slow down as his health deteriorated. In 1770 at the age of 56, Whitefield's asthmatic breathing worsened, but he continued to preach and travel with fervor. One day when a friend told him he was more fit to sleep than preach, this was his response:

"Lord Jesus, I am weary in Thy work, but not of it. If I have not finished my course, let me go and speak for Thee once more in the fields, and seal Thy truth, and come home and die."

That day, he had difficulty speaking, but paused in prayer, and then preached with God's strength for two hours. The next morning, he left this broken world, having finished the race strongly. God wants us to be steadfast, as well:

Therefore, my beloved brethren, be steadfast, immovable, always abounding in the work of the Lord, knowing that your labor is not in vain in the Lord.
1 Corinthians 15:58 (NKJV)

God can sustain us through any difficulty. Somehow, we look around and see what "normally" occurs in the world, forgetting that we are set apart by the God we serve. He performs miracles in our daily lives, as all things are possible through Him. Remember what happened to God's servant, Moses:

Moses was one hundred and twenty years old when he died. His eyes were not dim nor his natural vigor diminished.
Deuteronomy 34:7 (NKJV)

God's plan includes the number of our days. Moses lived a powerful 120 years, while Oswald Chambers, the author of "My Utmost for His Highest," died at 43. His devotional revealed depth way beyond his years, and was published seven years after his death. Because we are tied so strongly to this world, most Christians seem to be more concerned with how to stay here, rather than looking ahead to eternity worshiping our Savior! One interesting explanation of heaven describes a dog not allowed inside the master's house. Even though the dog never has seen the inside, he continues to scratch at the door. It is not because of the amenities inside that the dog wants in; instead, it is because of **who** is inside. No matter what heaven is like, we should yearn to be there because of **Who is there!**

We have grown accustomed to many amenities in our modern culture, particularly the time-saving devices of technology, which actually can increase our work loads rather than lessen them. For example, take the cell phone. In biblical times, the only way of contacting a neighbor or friend was by going to see them. From the mail system to the telegraph, this technology continued to change until the telephone made it much easier to keep in touch. Three decades ago, the answering machine brought us to a point when we did not have to be home to receive that message. A 2013 study by the United Nations, reported that of 7 billion people in the world, 6 billion had cell phones! Most people feel enslaved to their cell phones. Instead of allowing calls to go to voice mail, they must answer that call even in the middle of other important conversations, or business. It is more difficult to disconnect from the technological highway.

No wonder so many people feel burned out! There no longer is "down time," and God gave us the perfect example of His recommendation by creating the Sabbath. He wants us to rest, to unwind, to spend time sitting at His feet, to nourish the relationships with our familes, to disconnect from the noise all around us:

Be still, and know that I am God;
I will be exalted among the nations,
I will be exalted in the earth!
Psalm 46:10 (NKJV)

If we are going in our own directions, that burn-out may occur, but when we are following the LORD, we are operating under His power and provision. Knowing how His supernatural power even protected the shoes of His chosen people can inspire us to trust Him! He cares more for us than He does for our shoes! When the obstacles in front of us seem insurmountable, we need to remember that they only seem that way! God puts us into those situations to see how we will respond! Our choices are to throw in the towel, or take a bite of elephant, for we can eat an elephant one bite at a time. For inspiration, remember the news of the shoes of the Jews!

DISCUSSION QUESTIONS:

1. What is the greatest difficulty facing you presently? Have you prayed for God's will to be done, or for the obstacle to be removed? Pray with thoughts of the Garden of Gethsemane, where Jesus prayed that if it is was possible, for this cup to be removed. But above all, Jesus prayed for God's will. Our sins being placed upon His shoulders was the obstacle He was about to face. If that obstacle had been removed, none of us would have relationship with God. In our prayer, we should ask God to remind us that He has a perfect plan in each of our lives!
2. God performed many miracles in the Old Testament. Jesus performed many miracles in the New Testament. Does God still perform miracles today? Why or why not? Has God changed? In fact, is He capable of changing?
3. If God protected their sandals and clothing, what do you think He did for the bodies of the children of Israel? Do you think there were people in the exodus who had to be carried, other than infants? We often complain of being tired. Is this insulting to God, who gives us the strength to endure?
4. Is "burned out" a phrase that should not apply to a Christian? Is it more likely that we become burned out or rusted by the lack of

staying busy in the LORD's work?

5. Write down three ways that you can personally apply this verse concerning God's provision with the "shoes of the Jews."

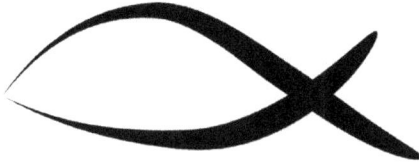

Notes:

Notes:

Notes:

Chapter 3,
David's Discernment

Perhaps no other book of the Bible approaches the depth and breadth of human emotion exhibited in the Book of Psalms, a compilation of Hebrew songs. Not surprisingly, the "man after God's own heart," King David, wrote at least 74 of the 150 Psalms, and 34 others have not been attributed to any author, so David may have written some of those, as well. He was the king that all other kings of Israel were measured against in 1 and 2 Kings and 1 and 2 Chronicles, though it was not because David was sinless. Instead, King David's most valuable asset appears to be his acknowledgment of his own sin, along with going to the LORD to ask forgiveness for that sin. There are many psalms that focus on men in the midst of trial. Lest we forget, the focus of each of those psalms can have multiple applications. Obviously, the most direct focus applies to the man writing the psalm within the particular circumstance he is facing. Secondly, those psalms also apply to each of us:

[16] All Scripture is given by inspiration of God, and is profitable for doctrine, for reproof, for correction, for instruction in

righteousness, [17] that the man of God may be complete, thoroughly equipped for every good work.
2 Timothy 3:16-17 (NKJV)

Also, many of those psalms depict the plight of the Jews prophetically, in the Great Tribulation. While we could spend the rest of this book studying the numerous psalms about trials, let's focus on Psalm 51. Before studying this psalm, let's review some important events in the life of King David.

By the time he was King in Jerusalem, David already had endured a battle with a giant, where David commented that the battle belonged to the LORD. As that battle occurred when David was still a lad, it is interesting to see if his trust in the LORD increased or decreased as David's power grew. Afterward, David played the lyre for King Saul, and married the king's daughter. When King Saul began to worry about David's potential, the misguided king spent years trying to capture and kill David. Saul was the people's king, but David became God's king, after King Saul died in battle with the Philistines. King David won many battles, and brought the Ark of the Covenant to Jerusalem. While we could remember many facets of David's life, we tend to focus on his sin rather than his strengths. One sin seems to be the first remembered by most.

With his army in battle in the spring, King David remained in Jerusalem. One night, he looked from his balcony and saw a beautiful woman bathing. After inquiring of her identity and discovering that she was the wife of Uriah the Hittite, one of King David's mighty men who was in battle at that moment, King David asked for the woman to be brought to him. Though David already had married multiple wives, he had to fulfill his lusts with that woman, and Bathsheba became pregnant. Desiring to disguise his sin, King David called Uriah home from battle. In David's plan, Uriah would sleep with Bathsheba and return to the battle. David planned that when the battle was over, and Uriah came home, his wife would be pregnant, but he would not know he was not the father of the child to be born. Instead, Uriah put a kink into King David's plans. Uriah refused to go home while his men were still facing battle. King David's deception increased. He wrote a note to Joab, his general, and gave the note to Uriah to carry. In that note was the order to place Uriah in the front lines of the fiercest battle, and then to withdraw his fellow soldiers that he may die at the hands of the enemy. Though King David did not place a knife through the heart of Uriah, the blood was directly on his hands! Bathsheba knew about the adultery, and Joab knew about the murder, but King David thought only he and the LORD knew the whole, sordid tale. By this time, David had married Bathsheba, and the LORD had not allowed the child to live. After the LORD's punishment, King David had certainly hoped to put this sin in the past. But then Nathan the prophet confronted him:

¹ Then the Lord sent Nathan to David. And he came to him, and said to him: "There were two men in one city, one rich and the other poor. ² The rich man had exceedingly many flocks and herds. ³ But the poor man had nothing, except one little ewe lamb which he had bought and nourished; and it grew up together with him and with his children. It ate of his own food and drank from his own cup and lay in his bosom; and it was like a daughter to him. ⁴ And a traveler came to the rich man, who refused to take from his own flock and from his own herd to prepare one for the wayfaring man who had come to him; but he took the poor man's lamb and prepared it for the man who had come to him."
⁵ So David's anger was greatly aroused against the man, and he said to Nathan, "As the Lord lives, the man who has done this shall surely die! ⁶ And he shall restore fourfold for the lamb, because he did this thing and because he had no pity."
⁷ Then Nathan said to David, "You are the man! Thus says the Lord God of Israel: 'I anointed you king over Israel, and I delivered you from the hand of Saul. ⁸ I gave you your master's house and your master's wives into your keeping, and gave you the house of Israel and Judah. And if that had been too little, I

also would have given you much more! ⁹ Why have you despised the commandment of the Lord, to do evil in His sight? You have killed Uriah the Hittite with the sword; you have taken his wife to be your wife, and have killed him with the sword of the people of Ammon. ¹⁰ Now therefore, the sword shall never depart from your house, because you have despised Me, and have taken the wife of Uriah the Hittite to be your wife.' ¹¹ Thus says the Lord: 'Behold, I will raise up adversity against you from your own house; and I will take your wives before your eyes and give them to your neighbor, and he shall lie with your wives in the sight of this sun. ¹² For you did it secretly, but I will do this thing before all Israel, before the sun.' "
2 Samuel 12:1-12 (NKJV)

This is an incredibly sad event in the life of a godly king. King David's perceived ethical outlook caused him much anger and righteous indignation when Nathan told the story of a deceitful man, but when Nathan revealed that the story was about King David, Bathsheba and Uriah the Hittite, King David's heart broke! With that background in mind, now let's review Psalm 51, as it is identified as King David's confession to the LORD after that confrontation by Nathan. In this psalm, King David asked for God's forgiveness, and our God of mercy granted that request. But though David received forgiveness, his sin carried many repurcussions. Though King David desperately wanted to build the LORD a permanent home in Jerusalem, that task was given to David's son Solomon. David tells us in his own words why he could not accomplish that task:

² Then King David rose to his feet and said, "Hear me, my brethren and my people: I had it in my heart to build a house of rest for the ark of the covenant of the Lord, and for the footstool of our God, and had made preparations to build it. ³ But God said to me, 'You shall not build a house for My name, because you have been a man of war and have shed

blood.'
1 Chronicles 28:2-3 (NKJV)

Furthermore, again look at the words of the LORD from Nathan the prophet,

¹⁰ Now therefore, the sword shall never depart from your house, because you have despised Me, and have taken the wife of Uriah the Hittite to be your wife.' ¹¹ Thus says the Lord: 'Behold, I will raise up adversity against you from your own house; and I will take your wives before your eyes and give them to your neighbor, and he shall lie with your wives in the sight of this sun. ¹² For you did it secretly, but I will do this thing before all Israel, before the sun.' "
2 Samuel 12:10-12 (NKJV)

The LORD's prophecy, as always, came to fruition. King David's son, Absalom, rose up against King David. In fact, David fled Jerusalem in Absalom's attempt to kill his father. The people turned on King David just as quickly, though he retained a small, loyal band of followers. War ensued between David's forces and Absalom's forces, and though David instructed Joab not to hurt Absalom, Joab disregarded that order and killed David's son. David never seemed to get past the loss of his son, seeing Absalom's failures as his own failures as a father. Though God selected Solomon as the king to succeed David, it is likely that David would have selected Absalom.

Remember, according to 1 Samuel 15:22, God does not want our sacrifice; He wants our obedience! Our LORD desires for us to come to Him with broken and contrite hearts. Now, let's look at Psalm 51, which beautifully depicts the words of a sinner, asking a sinless God for forgiveness.

To the Chief Musician. A Psalm of David When Nathan the Prophet Went to Him, After He Had Gone in to Bathsheba.

[1] Have mercy upon me, O God,
According to Your lovingkindness;
According to the multitude of Your tender mercies,
Blot out my transgressions.
[2] Wash me thoroughly from my iniquity,
And cleanse me from my sin.
[3] For I acknowledge my transgressions,
And my sin is always before me.
[4] Against You, You only, have I sinned,
And done this evil in Your sight—
That You may be found just when You speak,
And blameless when You judge.
[5] Behold, I was brought forth in iniquity,
And in sin my mother conceived me.
[6] Behold, You desire truth in the inward parts,
And in the hidden part You will make me to know wisdom.
[7] Purge me with hyssop, and I shall be clean;
Wash me, and I shall be whiter than snow.
[8] Make me hear joy and gladness,
That the bones You have broken may rejoice.
[9] Hide Your face from my sins,
And blot out all my iniquities.
[10] Create in me a clean heart, O God,
And renew a steadfast spirit within me.
[11] Do not cast me away from Your presence,
And do not take Your Holy Spirit from me.
[12] Restore to me the joy of Your salvation,
And uphold me by Your generous Spirit.
[13] Then I will teach transgressors Your ways,
And sinners shall be converted to You.
[14] Deliver me from the guilt of bloodshed, O God,
The God of my salvation,
And my tongue shall sing aloud of Your righteousness.
[15] O Lord, open my lips,
And my mouth shall show forth Your praise.
[16] For You do not desire sacrifice, or else I would give it;

You do not delight in burnt offering.
¹⁷ The sacrifices of God are a broken spirit,
A broken and a contrite heart—
These, O God, You will not despise.
¹⁸ Do good in Your good pleasure to Zion;
Build the walls of Jerusalem.
¹⁹ Then You shall be pleased with the sacrifices of
righteousness,
With burnt offering and whole burnt offering;
Then they shall offer bulls on Your altar.
Psalm 51:1-19 (NKJV)

What a beautiful prayer! Let's go through this verse-by-verse and try to observe what David was feeling after being confronted by Nathan. In verse one, David asks for God mercy. Mercy is not getting what we deserve, and is starkly contrasted with grace, which is getting what we do not deserve. Each of our sins earns death, but God shows us so much mercy! David then asks for God to cleanse him in verse two. Sometimes, we tend to forget how dirty sin makes us. We seem to rationalize our sin, and categorize it into "big sins" and "little sins." Guess what God calls a "white lie?" A lie! All sin is complicated and has far-reaching repercussions, reminiscent of "Oh, what a tangled web we weave when first we practice to deceive." When a man tells one lie, he must cover that lie with another lie, another sin. According to Romans, all of creation changed when Adam sinned. It is hard to envision how each sinful choice that we make adversely can affect the lives of others. If this seems unlikely, discuss it with the family of an alcoholic!

David says, **"For I acknowledge my transgressions, And my sin is always before me,"** in the third verse. When we claim not to be sinners, we are calling God a liar, according to 1 John 1:10. It is wonderful that God can forget our sin, but it is always before us. Verse four reminds us that our sin is against God. It is easy to see our sin as against our fellow man, but most of us seem to forget that each time we sin, we have joined forces with the enemy of God, Satan. Sin is a choice to fight for the enemy of God!

As David continues in the fifth verse, he reminds us that we are all born into sin from sinful parents. This could be interpreted as rationalization that because our parents are sinners and we carry their sin nature, we are going to sin, too. Yet David already had endured a period of rationalizing his sin involving Bathsheba and Uriah. Instead, he is acknowledging the stark difference between a man who cannot live perfectly and a God who cannot sin. What a chasm dwells between those two! Without a Mediator, each of us would be hopelessly destined for death and destruction!

According to verse six, God desires for truth to be inside of us. Most of us are more concerned with what is on the outside than what is on the inside. We must have the right clothes and the right car; from makeup to haircut to the perfect smile, we attend church wanting our fellow Christians to see that we are "blessed," somehow equating that holy word with earthly prosperity. Yet we are not much different than the white-washed sepulchers, the hypocritical Pharisees, as they were described by Jesus in Matthew 23:27. God desires to see our behavior reflecting the changes that He has made on the inside! A wise man once stated that character is whom we are when no one is watching. It is simple to parrot the words of the Bible, and much more difficult to live those words!

One of the best-known verses of this psalm occurs in verse seven, when David writes,

Purge me with hyssop, and I shall be clean;
Wash me, and I shall be whiter than snow.

"Whiter than snow" almost sounds like an impossibility. People who spend time on ski slopes certainly can testify to the snow-blindness that can occur when without goggles. The pure, bright whiteness of that snow can be dizzying! Imagine what it will be like to stand in the presence of Jesus. We think of the brightness of the sun, but there is no shadow in the presence of our Savior, as His light is everywhere! We have bloodstains from our sin, but only one thing can wash us white as snow—the blood of Jesus! In verse eight, we see that each of us should feel joy and gladness, even when the bones God has broken may rejoice. Think of King David. In the aftermath of his sin with Bathsheba, their son died. David's son from another wife rose up and tried to kill him. Once again, our sin has repercussions, and rather than mourn with the losses, we should rejoice in a God who loves us so much that He punishes us. A parent does not demonstrate love through leniency. Instead, punishment helps us to learn lessons that will become much more valuable down the road. Jesus reminded us in the Sermon on the Mount (Matthew 5:4) that **"blessed are those who mourn, for they shall be comforted."** We can be comforted that God sees everything we do and cares about everything we do!

In verse nine, David writes,

Hide Your face from my sins,
And blot out all my iniquities.

Once again, this is miraculous, that a God who knows everything can forget something. He chooses to forget our sin when we ask for His forgiveness. The Bible teaches us more than once about God's ability to completely release our sin:

As far as the east is from the west,
So far has He removed our transgressions from us.
Psalm 103:12 (NKJV)

He will again have compassion on us,
And will subdue our iniquities.
You will cast all our sins
Into the depths of the sea.
Micah 7:19 (NKJV)

**Indeed it was for my own peace
That I had great bitterness;
But You have lovingly delivered my soul from the pit of
corruption,
For You have cast all my sins behind Your back.
Isaiah 38:17 (NKJV)**

Our forgiven sins are on the ocean floor, covered in mud. How often do we dredge up those sins in our memories, though our Savior has promised us that He does not do that? Think of the phrase "forgive and forget." Truthfully, we are limited in our powers of forgiveness. We are capable of forgiving others, but mostly are incapable in regards to forgetting. It is difficult for us to comprehend how God knows everything, but does not remember our sin. He chooses not to remember our sin! Once He has dealt with our sin, it is gone. The moment He dealt with that sin was at the cross, when Jesus received the punishment that each of us earned and deserved. It seems like such a simple concept for us to acknowledge His action and ask for His forgiveness, but often, pride keeps us from admitting that we have failed once again. Notice that David does not just ask for God's forgiveness for the sin involving Uriah and Bathsheba, but for all sin. God is ready, willing and able to forgive all sin in all men! Talk about a miracle!

We can see another miracle in verses 10-12, also well-known verses.

**[10] Create in me a clean heart, O God,
And renew a steadfast spirit within me.
[11] Do not cast me away from Your presence,
And do not take Your Holy Spirit from me.
[12] Restore to me the joy of Your salvation,
And uphold me by Your generous Spirit.**

God created us, and in that creation, He created our hearts the first time. What makes us believe that He does not have the ability to

52

recreate those hearts? We can think of this in the physical way, as in the heart transplant of a surgeon. But what is even more important is that He can take our coldness and our hardness and fill our hearts with His love:

I will give you a new heart and put a new spirit within you; I will take the heart of stone out of your flesh and give you a heart of flesh.
Ezekiel 36:26 (NKJV)

At the same time, God does not wipe our memories clean and give us new brains. Instead, though He forgets our sins, we still can remember. God desires for us to use that memory of sin to praise Him for His mercy, grace and forgiveness, and to have compassion on others who are struggling in the same sins that He has delivered us from. Sadly, we often can be quicker to judgment than compassion, but instead of condemnation, we should see each sinner as being in the same position we were in before we received the forgiveness of our LORD Jesus! Simultaneously, He renews a steadfast spirit within us. Steadfast means unshakeable!

To correctly understand verse 11, we need to grasp the difference between the presence of the Holy Spirit in the Old Testament and His presence in the New Testament. In the Old Testament, God filled men with His Holy Spirit selectively for a specific ministry. On the other hand, when Jesus returned to heaven, He gave believers the gift of the Holy Spirit. He does not leave us! So we do not need to pray this portion of David's prayer, as He will not take His Holy Spirit from us once He has given us that gift!

In Verse 12, David asks the LORD to restore unto him the joy of salvation! What a glorious time it was when we stepped from a broken world into the arms of our Savior, who released us from the burden of sin and removed the debt of our sins. Sadly, we often forget what it was like in those days. Many of us carried our Bibles everywhere soon after accepting the LORD, hungry for every word. While each relationship is different, we often can resemble an old married couple, who no longer speak to each other, rather than that same couple when they were on their honeymoon. With the LORD, the honeymoon never has to end, as He desires for our intimacy with Him to continue to draw closer! We need to remember to return to the foot of the cross where it all began! Because of the forgiveness that David felt, and each of us should feel, verse 13 demonstrates the response that each of our lives should contain…**"I will teach transgressors Your ways and sinners shall be converted to You!"** David knows that the LORD has forgiven him. That brings joy. And joy is a megaphone to a world of sinners of what gift is available to them. Our actions speak much more loudly than our words when we are sharing the Gospel with unbelievers.

David asks for the LORD to deliver him from the guilt of bloodshed in verse 14. David was a bloody king and a warrior. We know that the bloodshed on David's hands caused God to disallow him from building the Temple in Jerusalem, with that duty passed to David's son, Solomon. Yet we do not know if it was the blood on David's hands from battle or from the indirect murder of Uriah, Bathsheba's husband. Look at this reflection upon the life of King David:

[4] Nevertheless for David's sake the Lord his God gave him a lamp in Jerusalem, by setting up his son after him and by establishing Jerusalem; [5] because David did what was right in the eyes of the Lord, and had not turned aside from anything that He commanded him all the days of his life, except in the matter of Uriah the Hittite.
1 Kings 15:4-5 (NKJV)

Just as King David did here, we are to sing of the LORD's righteousness. Paul reminds us in Romans that there is not one person who is righteous! This song continues in verse 15 with praise. That praise should emanate from our lips always! Verse 16 reminds us that God does not want our sacrifice; nor does He delight in our burnt offerings. Remember, God created the sacrificial system as a tutor, to demonstrate to the Jews that they would continue to sin. Sacrifices included much ritual and even more work, but also understand that each sacrifice involved the death of an innocent animal. We know that there can be no forgiveness of sins without the spilling of innocent blood. Sadly, people today are more concerned with shedding the blood of an innocent animal than shedding the blood of our innocent Savior!

Verse 17 highlights the sacrifices that God desires in His children, broken spirits and contrite hearts. If our sin would break our hearts in the same manner that our sin breaks God's heart, we would understand His desire. We want to move forward after each sin, but as stated above, though God forgives us, each sin has ramifications on our lives and the lives around us. Are we truly saddened by the fact that we sinned against God or more saddened by the consequences we may have to deal with? Think of the parental comment before spanking a child, "This is going to hurt me more than it is going to hurt you." God only wants the best for us, but the best often can be difficult days resulting from our bad choices. If we learn lessons from those choices, how can it be less than perfect? Finally, David wraps up this prayerful song by referring to God's holy city:

18 Do good in Your good pleasure to Zion;
Build the walls of Jerusalem.
19 Then You shall be pleased with the sacrifices of righteousness,
With burnt offering and whole burnt offering;
Then they shall offer bulls on Your altar.

The word "good" somehow does not seem good enough when used in reference to God, but that has more to do with our usage of that word. When we ask a man how he feels, and he says (like James Brown) that he feels good, we come up with the assessment that he does not feel bad, but also does not feel perfect. God is good, but God is not just fair to middling. God is above all, exceedingly, abundantly perfect! When David asks our good God to build the walls of Jerusalem, he is asking for God's protection, for a city with walls was easier to defend against enemies. A time is coming when Jerusalem will no longer need gates and walls; that is when Jesus comes in to rule and reign as the King of glory (Psalm 24). In the Millennium, there will be sacrifices again. That may not make any sense to us, as we know that our sins already have been covered by the blood of the Lamb, but sacrifices will occur as a memorial and testament to the LORD. Some symbols point forward, and this symbol will point backward, to a time that is past.

Since this book is about trials, we need to see this psalm in regard to enduring the trials of our lives. Job's friends erroneously attributed his trial to sin in his life. Though they were mistaken, sin often can be the cause of our trials. A great first step when enduring a trial is to reflect upon the sins in our lives. Confession is not a meeting with a priest, who assigns us a penalty of repeating a prayer numerous times. Instead, confession is acknowledging our sin to the God we sinned against.

⁹ If we confess our sins, He is faithful and just to forgive us our sins and to cleanse us from all unrighteousness. ¹⁰ If we say that we have not sinned, we make Him a liar, and His word is not in us.
1 John 1:9-10 (NKJV)

He does not cleanse us from some of the unrighteousness, but all of it! On *Yom Kippur*, the Day of Atonement, Jews reflect upon the sins they have committed in the past year. Because there is no longer a Temple to perform sacrifices, there is no innocent blood spilled to cover that sin. Instead, they meet in the synagogue, spend the day fasting, and grade their own lives with a spiritual abacus. One moral deed (*mitzvah* - מִצְוָה) performed as a religious duty, becomes one mark for the good while one sin becomes one mark for the bad. If a Jew can remember more good deeds than bad, he thinks he is a good man. But we do not get to judge ourselves; God is our judge, and by His rules, one sin makes a man worthy of death! Still, the present-day process of the Day of Atonement is one we all should practice. We need to look back at our sins and confess those sins. Let the cleansing begin today! (And it will not hurt to rinse, wash and repeat tomorrow!)

King David was not perfect, but we know him as a "man after God's own heart" because he understood and acknowledged that he was a sinner...and asked the LORD's forgiveness. It is not the sin in our lives that makes us dirty. It is the lack of acknowledgment of that sin. God can cleanse any of our dirtiness. What can wash away our sin? Nothing but the blood of Jesus!

Discussion Questions:

1. When God forgives us for our sins, and wipes the slate clean, can we still have to deal with the ramifications of that sin? Give examples.
2. In this chapter, we discussed some of the ramifications of sin in the life of King David. Give some examples of the ramifications of sin in the lives of other biblical characters. (Suggestions: Paul, Peter, Elijah, Jacob).
3. If God gives us new, clean hearts, why does He not give us new, clean minds?
4. Discuss how sin has damaged your life.
5. Though we all may walk difficult paths because of our sinful decisions, the best part of those paths is that we are never alone. Now, discuss some of the ways that Jesus has made you aware that He is with you in the midst of every trial, just as He danced with Shadrach, Meshach and Abednego in the fiery furnace of Daniel.

Notes:

Notes:

Notes:

Chapter 4,
Job's Journey!

Even the secular world is familiar with "the patience of Job," at least in terminology. Yet the resonating lessons from this Old Testament book can be some of the most helpful for anyone enduring trials. Job helps us to answer some of the most challenging questions.

1. Why is this happening?
2. Is God punishing me for my sin?
3. When will the trial end?
4. What am I supposed to do?

Many people erroneously believe that the Book of Job teaches us why righteous people suffer, but truly, the Book of Job does not give that reason. Nor will this book. Instead, what we should learn is that God does not cause a believer's suffering, yet He always remains with us in our trials! Most of the time, He carries us! Let's review some of the highlights of the Book of Job, which likely was written before any other book of the Bible, or at the same time as the *Torah*.

Job begins with an interesting exchange between Satan and God. At one time, Satan had been the ranking angel of heaven according to Isaiah 14 and Ezekiel 28, but spearheaded a rebellion involving one-third of the angels. He and his followers had been cast out of heaven. At the beginning of the Book of Job, Satan had returned to heaven and stood before the throne of God. This is an interesting nugget on its own, that a fallen angel in rebellion against God is still welcome before God's throne! We see that Satan had not remained in heaven; instead, he had been walking to and fro on the earth. What had he been doing? Certainly, he was busy in the same trickery and deceit that he employs today, while trying to make believers stumble. If Satan cannot pry us out of God's hands when we are His, then why does the great deceiver even bother fighting this battle over and over again? Though Satan cannot affect our salvation, he can ruin our testimonies, which in turn, can affect the salvation of others. Additionally, it has to eat at him to see God's followers filled with joy. Job was one of the most joyful men on the earth. God described Job with glowing terms when speaking to Satan:

Then the Lord said to Satan, "Have you considered My servant Job, that there is none like him on the earth, a blameless and upright man, one who fears God and shuns evil?" Job 1:8 (NKJV)

Any of us would be tickled pink for the LORD to refer to us as lovingly. Satan, filled with arrogance, told the LORD that the only reason Job walked so blamelessly was that his life was completely blessed. To prove his point, Satan requested that God remove the hedge of protection from Job. This is not a 6-foot high hedge separating one yard from another in the suburbs! We may picture a towering maze, impossible to maneuver. This hedge of protection made it impossible for Satan to bother Job in any way. Certainly, we all can envision a hedge of protection in each of our lives. It is simple when thinking of the past to remember times when we must have had a guardian angel keeping us from harm or death. Other than the mere existence of this hedge is the knowledge that it can be removed! When God removed the hedge of protection from Job, Satan had his way with Job, though God would not allow Satan to touch a hair on Job's head. So Satan, trying to prove his point, began by having marauders steal all of Job's oxen and donkeys. At the same time, the marauders killed many of his servants. While the servant who brought the news was still speaking, another arrived and told of a second tragedy. Fire fell from heaven and burned up all Job's sheep, and killed more servants. Moments later, another servant arrived to say that Job's camels also had been stolen, and more servants killed. Finally, a fourth servant came with the most devastating news. Job's seven sons and three daughters all were celebrating in the same home, and a great wind from heaven killed them all.

Emphatically, that fire and great wind from heaven were not from God, but from Satan. In a few moments, Job had lost 7,000 sheep, 3,000 camels, 500 yoke of oxen, 500 female donkeys, most of his servants and 10 children. His response should remind us why God spoke of Job in such glowing terms:

20 Then Job arose, tore his robe, and shaved his head; and he fell to the ground and worshiped. 21 And he said: "Naked I came from my mother's womb, And naked shall I return there. The Lord gave, and the Lord has taken away; Blessed be the name of the Lord." 22 In all this Job did not sin nor charge God with wrong. Job 1:20-22 (NKJV)

It is difficult to fathom the arrogance of Satan. God created him as the angel Lucifer (meaning "morning star" or "light bearer" in Hebrew), and he served God in heaven. How could Satan not know or completely understand the omniscience, omnipotence and omnipresence of God? When we see anyone in God's presence in the Bible, they are flat on their faces. Unlike the chorus from the

Christian song, "I Can Only Imagine," it is only in the imagination that we will stand in His presence when confronted with His perfection. When the apostle John was in the Spirit on the LORD's day and found himself in heaven in Revelation 1, instead of walking closely with Jesus as he did on this earth, John took another approach:

17 And when I saw Him, I fell at His feet as dead. But He laid His right hand on me, saying to me, "Do not be afraid; I am the First and the Last. 18 I am He who lives, and was dead, and behold, I am alive forevermore. Amen. And I have the keys of Hades and of Death. 19 Write the things which you have seen, and the things which are, and the things which will take place after this.
Revelation 1:17-19 (NKJV)

Satan remains filled with that pride and arrogance now. When we are filled with pride, we are reflecting Satan; when we are filled with humility, we are reflecting Jesus! That pride will become humility for all, as every knee shall bow and every tongue confess that Jesus Christ is LORD (Philippians 2:10-11). In these prophetic verses from Isaiah 14, we see Satan's future:

12 "How you are fallen from heaven,
O Lucifer, son of the morning!
How you are cut down to the ground,
You who weakened the nations!
13 For you have said in your heart:
'I will ascend into heaven,
I will exalt my throne above the stars of God;
I will also sit on the mount of the congregation
On the farthest sides of the north;
14 I will ascend above the heights of the clouds,
I will be like the Most High.'
15 Yet you shall be brought down to Sheol,
To the lowest depths of the Pit.
Isaiah 14:12-15 (NKJV) 64

Whether his pride does not allow him to see this future (as Satan certainly knows God's Word better than most Christians), or he realizes that he is operating on borrowed time is another discussion, entirely. Yet we can see that even Satan is not arrogant enough to believe he ever could be more glorious than God. In verse 14 above, he verbally placed himself on the same level, but not higher, when saying, "I will be like the Most High." A simple comparison between God, who few serve, and Satan, who many serve, is in order. God, who is the Most High, seeks to elevate each of us to a relationship with Him. Yet Satan, desiring to be like the Most High, desires to step on each of us on his way to the top. Most of us have encountered people who believe it makes them better or more powerful when destroying someone else, either mentally or physically. In the case of Job, Satan failed at destroying Job mentally, and then returned to the throne of God to ask for more leeway. Next, Satan wanted to prove to God that if he could hurt Job physically, Job would no longer seek and follow the LORD. To new believers, this can be a problematic section of the Bible, as it almost appears to be a bet between God and Satan. If God is truly omniscient, then why did He allow this to happen when He already knew the outcome? And if He knew the outcome, why did God allow Job's children to die, the servants to die, and allow Satan to hurt his most blameless follower on the earth?

[8] **"For My thoughts are not your thoughts,
Nor are your ways My ways," says the Lord.**
[9] **"For as the heavens are higher than the earth,
So are My ways higher than your ways,
And My thoughts than your thoughts.
Isaiah 55:8-9 (NKJV)**

It may seem like a bet, but do not be fooled. God would not fall for any of Satan's traps, and every action fits into God's intricate plan. Additionally, each life is precious to God, including the lives of Job's children and Job's servants. Yet God is most concerned with our eternal lives. Trials and difficulties in earthly lives are more of a ways to a means. As we return to Job, we see that God acceded to Satan's devious request, though God would not allow Satan to kill Job. Job endured incredible pain, endured an unsupporting wife who encouraged her husband to **"curse God and die,"** and finally, endured three of his best friends who came to support Job by spending many days accusing him of hidden sin and its resulting punishment. Bildad was probably the most insensitive and insulting. After Job lost all 10 of his children, Bildad said,

[18] He is driven from light into darkness,
And chased out of the world.
[19] He has neither son nor posterity among his people,
Nor any remaining in his dwellings.
[20] Those in the west are astonished at his day,
As those in the east are frightened.
[21] Surely such are the dwellings of the wicked,
And this is the place of him who does not know God."
Job 18:18-21 (NKJV)

Job displayed his patience and godliness by not punching Bildad in the nose, as bringing up a situation where a man does not have a son soon after seven were killed is not only insensitive, but cruel. Is it possible that God could judge a sinful man by destroying his family? Yes, but it is not our job to speak for God, though Job's three "friends" must have felt invited to take that position. God certainly is capable of speaking for Himself. Today, we can find ourselves in much different situations when comforting our suffering friends. With the Holy Spirit within each believer and the gift of the Bible, God often brings to mind relative Bible verses that can encourage a fellow believer. This event in the Book of Job occurred before there was a written Bible! Instead of comforting Job with God's Word, these three pounded him with their own thoughts. Their language might be articulate and poetic, but their words were empty in application to Job's life. Many of the comments made by Job's friends, Eliphaz, Bildad and Zophar, were eloquent, and even could be correct in many circumstances. But all three were completely wrong in the case of Job. Sadly, while they were accusing Job of sin, they were all sinning by speaking for God. Though Job's children all were killed, it is easy to see why Satan had not killed Job's wife or his friends Larry, Moe and Curly. All four seemed to be fighting for Satan in this battle, or at least he used them for his purposes.

Job did sin in the midst of this situation, as he fell into some prideful righteousness. Frustrated and angry, Job repeatedly expressed his desire to question God. He got his chance! Five of the most powerful chapters in the Bible are Job 38-42, where God answered Job. Let's get a glimpse at the beginning:

2 "Who is this who darkens counsel
By words without knowledge?
3 Now prepare yourself like a man;
I will question you, and you shall answer Me.
4 "Where were you when I laid the foundations of the earth?
Tell Me, if you have understanding.
Job 38:2-4 (NKJV)

This section in the Book of Job tells us more about creation than Genesis. In God's opening statement to Job, He speaks of darkening counsel "by words without knowledge." If we have the intellect of Albert Einstein, it is nothing in comparison to a Creator who knows EVERYTHING! How can we ever question God? Yet most of us have, especially in difficult times. Notice that in the finale of Job, all of his possessions are returned in a way:

67

Job's "Possessions:"

Beginning of the Book of Job	Ending of the Book of Job	Change
7,000 Sheep	14,000 Sheep	Doubled
3,000 Camels	6,000 Camels	Doubled
500 Yoke of Oxen	1,000 Yoke of Oxen	Doubled
500 Female Donkeys	1,000 Female Donkeys	Doubled
7 Sons	7 Sons	Same
3 Daughters	3 Daughters	Same

Why did God double all of Job's possessions, except for his children? Animals are earthly, but a strong guess is that all 20 of Job's children will be with him in heaven. So when looked at through a heavenly perspective, God also doubled that blessing. It is a bigger miracle that Job continued to have relations with his wife after she encouraged her husband to "curse God and die!" Instead Job responded with one of the most poignant statements ever uttered by a Christian man:

Though He slay me, yet will I trust Him.
Job 13:15 (NKJV)

So let's get back to those questions that the Book of Job seems to answer that we mentioned at the beginning of this chapter:

1. Why is this happening?
In the case of Job, and in the case of God's relationship with any of His children, God desires to draw us closer to Him. We grow much more when under fire. That is the same way precious metals are purified. We know that Hebrews 12:29 reminds us that our God is a consuming fire, and fortunately for Christians, he consumes our sins, rather than us! Let's read about His furnace:

9 "For My name's sake I will defer My anger,

And for My praise I will restrain it from you,
So that I do not cut you off.
[10] Behold, I have refined you, but not as silver;
I have tested you in the furnace of affliction.
[11] For My own sake, for My own sake, I will do it;
For how should My name be profaned?
And I will not give My glory to another.
Isaiah 48:9-11 (NKJV)

That furnace of affliction is for God's name's sake. He has made
promises to us that are not based upon our performance. Instead,
those promises rely on His holiness. If He broke any of His
promises to us, God would no longer be holy or righteous. His
name is holy! Our God is an awesome God, who protects His
children, and sometimes punishes them. Peter, who denied the
LORD the night before His crucifixion, certainly understood the
difficulty of trials. He had this to say:

[6] In this you greatly rejoice, though now for a little while, if
need be, you have been grieved by various trials, [7] that the
genuineness of your faith, being much more precious than gold
that perishes, though it is tested by fire, may be found to praise,
honor, and glory at the revelation of Jesus Christ, [8] whom
having not seen you love. Though now you do not see Him, yet
believing, you rejoice with joy inexpressible and full of glory, [9]
receiving the end of your faith—the salvation of your souls.
1 Peter 1:6-9 (NKJV)

The genuineness of our faith is tested by fire, and that testing
reveals the end result of our salvation. Instead of complaining or
grieving through our trials, we should be rejoicing! If those trials
are brought on by our own sin, we can deal with that by asking
for God's forgiveness, and walking away from our sin. If instead,
those trials come as result of a spiritual battle with Satan and his
legion of demons, we also should rejoice, as God would only allow
that for His purposes. Satan is not going to mess with someone

unless they are doing something right for God. Those battles and attacks should remind us that we are on the right path! Also remember that God allowed the trial; if it is a difficult one, He must have great confidence in us to allow us to succeed in such a difficult situation! We need those trials to grow closer to the LORD. Remember if a mountain was smooth, we could not climb it!

2. Is God punishing me for my sin?

Some pastors spend most of their sermons discussing God's punishment, just as Job's friends were certain that his affliction was because of secret sin in his life. Yes, God does punish His children, but do not forget that He is slow to anger. All it takes is a little self-reflection and memory to some sins of our pasts to see that God did not punish us as harshly as we would have punished someone else in the same situation! Additionally, when Christians sin, we rarely see instantaneous punishment. Certainly, Job endured many days of his own self-reflection, but could not attribute any unrepented sin that might have caused his affliction. Though he overlooked some self-righteous pride, most of that was the result of his discussion with Eliphaz, Bildad and Zophar. When dealing with a trial, it is always a great first step to ask the LORD for His forgiveness for the sins in our lives. Yet do not equate a trial with sin! Jesus reminded us:

These things I have spoken to you, that in Me you may have peace. In the world you will have tribulation; but be of good cheer, I have overcome the world."
John 16:33 (NKJV)

3. When will the trial end?

This might be the most difficult issue. We do not know when it will end, but we do know that it will. Some trials end with death, exemplified by Jesus, and also by Stephen. Yet if God calls us to be martyrs, He certainly prepares us for the task and will remain with us throughout. Stephen looked into heaven as he was being stoned and echoed similar words of Jesus,

Then he knelt down and cried out with a loud voice, "Lord, do not charge them with this sin." And when he had said this, he fell asleep.
Acts 7:60 (NKJV)

Most of our trials, though, do not end in martyrdom. Satan hates us because we serve the risen Christ, and Satan certainly hates Jesus. Consequently, we are his enemies, as well. Jesus said,

[18] "If the world hates you, you know that it hated Me before it hated you. [19] If you were of the world, the world would love its own. Yet because you are not of the world, but I chose you out of the world, therefore the world hates you. [20] Remember the word that I said to you, 'A servant is not greater than his master.' If they persecuted Me, they will also persecute you. If they kept My word, they will keep yours also.
John 15:18-20 (NKJV)

As believers, we should continue to focus on two aspects of persecution. First, we should be praying for our Christian brothers and sisters in harm's way because of their beliefs and secondly, we should be thankful for where God has us. That does not mean we should expect our lives to be easy. Corrie Ten Boom comes to mind. Her family protected many Jews in the Netherlands during World War II. After saving many lives, the Nazis imprisoned the Ten Booms in concentration camps before the war ended. Corrie Ten Boom survived the holocaust and said this:

"You will never feel that Jesus is everything you need until Jesus is everything you have."

If we are focusing on money, food, possessions and the like, we lose sight of God's sufficiency in our lives. Take away the money, the food and the possessions and give us His grace! As the LORD told Paul, when Paul asked that the thorn in his flesh be removed:

And He said to me, "My grace is sufficient for you, for My strength is made perfect in weakness."
2 Corinthians 12:9 (NKJV)

Another Ten Boom, Corrie's sister Betsie, who died in the Ravensbruck concentration camp, said:

"There is no pit so deep that God's love is not deeper still."

If we are in a pit, know that God's love can find us there just as easily. In fact, God's love can find us there more easily, for it is in those pits that we know we cannot rely on ourselves and we are forced to acknowledge that He is the only one who can save us. Some have noted that there are no atheists in foxholes!

Any trial will end when God desires for it to end. He has a result in mind! In the case of Job, that result was an increased closeness in their relationship. God typically has more than one result on His mind, and is not limited.

[6] Be anxious for nothing, but in everything by prayer and supplication, with thanksgiving, let your requests be made known to God; [7] and the peace of God, which surpasses all understanding, will guard your hearts and minds through Christ Jesus.
Philippians 4:6-7 (NKJV)

Peace in the midst of ease does not surpass understanding. In fact, that kind of peace is expected. Yet when we exhibit peace in the midst of turmoil, it points to God's presence in our lives. It is that kind of peace that speaks loudly to unbelievers, demonstrating a supernatural presence in our lives. In that way, trials can open deep conversations that can plant seeds in the lives of unbelievers. Often, God uses our trials for His kingdom building. With all that

He has given us already, even if we had to suffer for 70 years, it would be worth it all. Yet God demonstrates His mercy, giving us rest. Jesus said,

[28] Come to Me, all you who labor and are heavy laden, and I will give you rest. [29] Take My yoke upon you and learn from Me, for I am gentle and lowly in heart, and you will find rest for your souls. [30] For My yoke is easy and My burden is light."
Matthew 11:28-30 (NKJV)

Be patient in the middle of trials and remember that patience is a fruit of the Holy Spirit. The trial will end, either with His rest, or we will find ourselves in the arms of our Savior. He is holding us during the trial, too!

4. What am I supposed to do?

As 1 Thessalonians 5:17 reminds us, pray without ceasing! But most importantly, what should we pray for? How about for the trial to end? Personally, this seems like a dangerous request, as if God had a desired result, we likely would find ourselves in exactly the same situation again. When Jesus was about to endure the cross, He prayed!

He went a little farther and fell on His face, and prayed, saying, "O My Father, if it is possible, let this cup pass from Me; nevertheless, not as I will, but as You will."
Matthew 26:39 (NKJV)

In prayer, Jesus asked the Father for another solution, but most importantly, included a clause that whatever happened would be in God's perfect will. What He was about to endure was separation from the Father for the only time in all of eternity. Jesus not only carried our sins, but became sin for us (2 Corinthians 5:21)! We worry about the loss of a job, a missed mortgage payment or a multitude of other meaningless issues. Instead, we should pray for contentment, peace in the midst of

73

turmoil, closeness with the LORD, to be used by Him, or for others to see Him in the midst of our trial.

One of the greatest non-biblical statements is to not major in the minors. It is difficult to see that everything else pales in comparison to the gift of salvation that Jesus already has given to believers. Job endured more than any, and God displayed His mercy and love. A neighbor once said that his difficulties were much worse than those Job endured, but there was not a Bible book named after the neighbor, nor was he ever mentioned as a blameless and upright man. Contentment in all things is the greatest lesson! God is not out to destroy His followers. Instead, know that His gifts are perfect, even if we do not have the spiritual sight to see or understand:

[11] If a son asks for bread from any father among you, will he give him a stone? Or if he asks for a fish, will he give him a serpent instead of a fish? [12] Or if he asks for an egg, will he offer him a scorpion? [13] If you then, being evil, know how to give good gifts to your children, how much more will your heavenly Father give the Holy Spirit to those who ask Him!" Luke 11:11-12 (NKJV)

DISCUSSION QUESTIONS:

1. When enduring trials, as all of us will, what is a perfect first step?
2. Part of the lesson here is how to trust in God during a trial, while another part is how to encourage others in their trials. What can we learn from Job's friends? How did God deal with them?
3. Trials come from God, but we can see in this chapter that Satan can have a part in those trials. Certainly, his heart is not to help us. What does that tell us about the sovereignty of God?

4. Job's wife was another interesting character in this story, who encouraged her husband to curse God and die! Possibly, there is not anyone who can help us as much as a spouse or hurt us as deeply. Give an example of a time when you could have helped, but caused more pain, in the trial of someone dear to you.

5. Job was a righteous man, but when defending himself to his friends, fell into sinful self-righteousness. At times, he spoke as if God needed to answer to him, though that sentiment changed when God spoke to him. Is it futile to argue with God? It certainly points to pride. Is God trying to teach us humility in every trial?

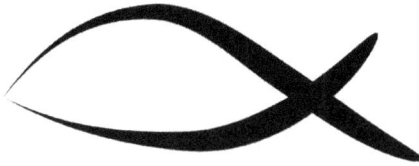

Notes:

Chapter 5,
Paul's Prudence

One of the reasons that trials can have such a hold on us is that we are so strongly tied to this earth. A Christian adage says, "Don't be so heavenly minded that you are no earthly good," but truly, that is not biblical. Instead, it should be more of a conditional statement. If we are heavenly minded, then we will be earthly good. Heavenly-minded people realize that nothing can separate us from God! The stronger our ties to this earth are, the more Satan can place in his arsenal of attack. Our greatest difficulties can go hand-in-hand with our greatest strengths. One example would be a godly marriage. When a husband loves his wife so deeply that he cannot envision life without her, suddenly he is tied strongly to this world and the things of this world. Paul wrote:

² Set your mind on things above, not on things on the earth. ³ For you died, and your life is hidden with Christ in God. ⁴ When Christ who is our life appears, then you also will appear with Him in glory.
Colossians 3:2-4 (NKJV)

This verse does not tell us that our families are not important. Instead, it is all about priority. First, we must focus on that relationship with God! It is amazing that the God who created all desires a relationship with us, to begin with! When we focus on Him, the rest of our lives fall into balance much more easily.

The problem occurs when we focus on the world, rather than heaven. It is easy to do when we rely on our senses, what we can grasp, smell, taste, see and hear. Instead, God wants us to center ourselves on the work He has set aside for each of us. Rather than worrying about provisions, if we are busy in the Lord's work, He certainly will provide! Miraculously, He provides all we need, often in the hour we need it! Our treasures are not here!

[19] "Do not lay up for yourselves treasures on earth, where moth and rust destroy and where thieves break in and steal; [20] but lay up for yourselves treasures in heaven, where neither moth nor rust destroys and where thieves do not break in and steal. [21] For where your treasure is, there your heart will be also. Matthew 6:19-21 (NKJV)

Money is not the only stumbling block that trips us. Idolatry is anything that gets in the way of our relationship with God. Sadly, all of us stumble along these lines. Often, the earthly treasure even can be a person, who we love so much that we cannot envision life without them. Yet no matter how special that love can be, it cannot compare to a heavenly life of dwelling with the Lord! Whenever God desires for us to join Him, it will be the perfect time!

Our challenge is how to dwell in a godly manner in a world that does not honor God. We still can honor Him in all we do! That includes all of our relationships – within our families, at school, at work, at church and at play! Even when we are confronted with people who do not believe in God, we remain His representatives. Additionally, we should make a special effort with strangers and aliens, for we are aliens on this earth, as well. Store up treasures in heaven, for the Bank of God gives much better interest! He remains interested in us! Many Christians are more concerned with living well on this earth, and do not even think of heaven. All sin will be gone, all temptation will be gone, all pain will be gone and all sadness will be gone. Wow, should we not want that? Most of us have heard Christians make comments along the lines of, "I am not ready to go to heaven yet. I want to get married and have children first." Certainly, those are not odd desires, but we must remember that God already has set the number of days each of us will live. King Hezekiah comes to mind.

¹ In those days Hezekiah was sick and near death. And Isaiah the prophet, the son of Amoz, went to him and said to him, "Thus says the Lord: 'Set your house in order, for you shall die and not live.' "
² Then Hezekiah turned his face toward the wall, and prayed to the Lord, ³ and said, "Remember now, O Lord, I pray, how I have walked before You in truth and with a loyal heart, and have done what is good in Your sight." And Hezekiah wept bitterly.
⁴ And the word of the Lord came to Isaiah, saying, ⁵ "Go and tell Hezekiah, 'Thus says the Lord, the God of David your father: "I have heard your prayer, I have seen your tears; surely I will add to your days fifteen years. ⁶ I will deliver you and this city from the hand of the king of Assyria, and I will defend this city." ' ⁷ And this is the sign to you from the Lord, that the Lord will do this thing which He has spoken: ⁸ Behold, I will bring the shadow on the sundial, which has gone down with the sun on the sundial of Ahaz, ten degrees backward." So the sun returned ten degrees on the dial by which it had gone down.
Isaiah 38:1-8 (NKJV)

God answered the prayer of Hezekiah, who did not feel he was ready to leave this earth, and gave Hezekiah 15 more years of life on earth. Yet what happened in that time frame is eye-opening.

When King Hezekiah finally died, his son Manasseh became king at the age of 12. Yes, Manasseh was born 3 years after King Hezekiah was to die on God's time schedule. Let's read about what King Manasseh did for Israel and Jerusalem:

¹ **Manasseh was twelve years old when he became king, and he reigned fifty-five years in Jerusalem. His mother's name was Hephzibah. ² And he did evil in the sight of the Lord, according to the abominations of the nations whom the Lord had cast out before the children of Israel. ³ For he rebuilt the high places which Hezekiah his father had destroyed; he raised up altars for Baal, and made a wooden image, as Ahab king of Israel had done; and he worshiped all the host of heaven and served them. ⁴ He also built altars in the house of the Lord, of which the Lord had said, "In Jerusalem I will put My name." ⁵ And he built altars for all the host of heaven in the two courts of the house of the Lord. ⁶ Also he made his son pass through the fire, practiced soothsaying, used witchcraft, and consulted spiritists and mediums. He did much evil in the sight of the Lord, to provoke Him to anger. ⁷ He even set a carved image of Asherah that he had made, in the house of which the Lord had said to David and to Solomon his son, "In this house and in Jerusalem, which I have chosen out of all the tribes of Israel, I will put My name forever; ⁸ and I will not make the feet of Israel wander anymore from the land which I gave their fathers—only if they are careful to do according to all that I have commanded them, and according to all the law that My servant Moses commanded them." ⁹ But they paid no attention, and Manasseh seduced them to do more evil than the nations whom the Lord had destroyed before the children of Israel.**
¹⁰ **And the Lord spoke by His servants the prophets, saying,**
¹¹ **"Because Manasseh king of Judah has done these abominations (he has acted more wickedly than all the Amorites who were before him, and has also made Judah sin with his idols), ¹² therefore thus says the Lord God of Israel: 'Behold, I am bringing such calamity upon Jerusalem and**

Judah, that whoever hears of it, both his ears will tingle. [13] And I will stretch over Jerusalem the measuring line of Samaria and the plummet of the house of Ahab; I will wipe Jerusalem as one wipes a dish, wiping it and turning it upside down. [14] So I will forsake the remnant of My inheritance and deliver them into the hand of their enemies; and they shall become victims of plunder to all their enemies, [15] because they have done evil in My sight, and have provoked Me to anger since the day their fathers came out of Egypt, even to this day.' "

2 Kings 21:1-15 (NKJV)

We serve a God who continues to answer the prayers of His children. One of the lessons each of us should learn is to pray like Jesus. Not my will be done, but Your will be done, Father! God's plan is perfect for each of us, and praying for His will to be done involves trust…that He cares for us so deeply and His plan is for our good and His glory. What is a better measure of our heavenly-mindedness than a simple clock? Each person walking this earth has the same 24 hours in each day. Having added all of the time-saving devices of technology to our lives seems to have complicated our lives more rather than giving us more time! Sadly, we have entered the Facebook and Twitter generation. Instead of depth, comments contain little necessary information. People have grown so accustomed to these snippets of information that sitting down and reading an entire chapter of the Bible in one sitting seems burdensome!

At the same time, we fill every minute of every day with busy-ness, instead of being concerned with the LORD's business. This is reminiscent of Martha in Luke 10, who felt overwhelmed in various preparations with Jesus in her house, while her sister Mary sat at the feet of Jesus and worshiped. Martha was offended that Mary would not help her, and attempted to get Jesus on her side. Instead, Jesus noticed the heart of Mary:

[41] **And Jesus answered and said to her, "Martha, Martha, you**

81

are worried and troubled about many things. ⁴² But one thing is needed, and Mary has chosen that good part, which will not be taken away from her."
Luke 10:41-42 (NKJV)

It is difficult to be Mary in a Martha world, but that aptly describes a challenge in most of our lives. God desires for us to take care of our families, and that includes both earning a living and spending time with them. It is a balance that can be starkly contrasted with the lives most of us live. Work becomes the top priority, and we work so hard that instead of attending church on Sunday morning, we sleep, because we "need" the rest. What would we do if we did not make as much money in our jobs? Would God still provide? Often, we have become so jaded by the world that surrounds us that we seem to be following a false God of earthly prosperity. God did not promise ease, earthly riches or the ability to purchase anything we ever dreamed to own. Instead, He promised to fulfill our needs and most importantly, He promised heavenly prosperity.

King David wrote multiple psalms asking why the wicked prosper, but the given in that question is that not all followers of the LORD seem to prosper. In Psalm 37, David writes, **"¹Do not fret because of evildoers, nor be envious of the workers of iniquity. ² For they shall soon be cut down like the grass, and wither as the green herb,"** and he continues, **"¹⁶ A little that a righteous man has is better than the riches of many wicked.¹⁷ For the arms of the wicked shall be broken, but the Lord upholds the righteous."** If we spend ample time studying God's Word, praying, and loving others, as a priority in our lives, then God certainly will bless and take care of our jobs, too. Again, by God's blessing upon our careers, that does not mean that we are going to become wealthy. That is a lie straight from the pit of hell.

Politics can become another hornet's nest for Christians. Regardless of the political party in the presidential office in the

United States, or which party controls the House and the Senate, God is still sovereign, and He is still on the throne. One pastor made a statement that through the unity of the Holy Spirit, all Christians always will vote for the same man, which is one of the most ridiculous statements ever uttered. What if some Christians are not listening, and the "wrong" man becomes the president? Does their lack of attentiveness to God change His will? God appoints kings and countries, according to Daniel 2:21. God's will includes blessings and curses, the rise of nations and the fall of nations. Somehow, many Christians believe that the United States is a blessed nation and the LORD never will remove that blessing. But reflect upon the fact that as a nation, this country no longer follows the Bible. It has removed prayer from the schools. Homosexuality is not only prevalent, but becoming as accepted as a Christian marriage (if not more so)! Heterosexual couples almost pervasively live together before marriage, and even more do not believe in marriage. Drug usage and crime continue to spiral out of control. 10% of Americans now claim to be atheists, with most of those being under 30-years-old. Does it sound like God is still the focus of the United States? Instead of "God Bless America," maybe we should focus more upon, "America Bless God!"

**[18] For many walk, of whom I have told you often, and now tell you even weeping, that they are the enemies of the cross of Christ: [19] whose end is destruction, whose god is their belly, and whose glory is in their shame—who set their mind on earthly things. [20] For our citizenship is in heaven, from which we also eagerly wait for the Savior, the Lord Jesus Christ, [21] who will transform our lowly body that it may be conformed to His glorious body, according to the working by which He is able even to subdue all things to Himself.
Philippians 3:18-21 (NKJV)**

If our citizenship is in the heavens, what keeps us so focused upon this earth? Retirement portfolios will not change our heavenly standing. In fact, it is God who has the best retirement package!

That earthly-focus likely comes from the fact that the earth is all we know. It is tangible. We can see it, smell it, taste it, hear it and feel it! Yet with spiritual eyes, heaven can be just as real to us! Many mistakenly think of the boredom associated with sitting on a cloud playing a harp, yet that is not the promise of heaven given us in the Bible. One way to change that focus is to spend more time with Jesus! A dear friend once suggested, "Tithe your time." Most of us are overly concerned with finances, and are not giving cheerfully. But what if we gave cheerfully of a much more precious commodity than money, our time? 10% of that 24-hour period is 2.4 hours. Even if we want to give the LORD 10% of our waking hours, that is still 1.5 hours a day. How many Christians actually do this? How many pastors even do this? How can we have a loving, viable relationship with anyone without giving that person time? We cannot know the LORD without giving Him time!

Trials seem to magnify when focus is on self. We always seem to want more. Think of the Jews in the wilderness, right after God parted the Red Sea. Days later, they were creating a golden calf to worship! "I know what you did for me, God, but what are You going to do for me now?" As idiotic as that event seems to us, we are no different. Trials magnify when we are steeped in discontentment. How did Paul summarize this for us?

[7] But what things were gain to me, these I have counted loss for Christ. [8] Yet indeed I also count all things loss for the excellence of the knowledge of Christ Jesus my Lord, for whom I have suffered the loss of all things, and count them as rubbish, that I may gain Christ [9] and be found in Him, not having my own righteousness, which is from the law, but that which is through faith in Christ, the righteousness which is from God by faith; [10] that I may know Him and the power of His resurrection, and the fellowship of His sufferings, being conformed to His death, [11] if, by any means, I may attain to the resurrection from the dead.

Philippians 3:7-11 (NKJV)

By the world's standards, Paul had much to boast about before coming to the LORD. Part of that was his heritage, a Jew of the tribe of Benjamin, educated by the respected Rabbi Gamaliel, a Pharisee. The tribe of Benjamin was centered in Jerusalem. Additionally, Paul's lineage could be traced back to Abraham. Before becoming a Christian, Paul had zealously persecuted Christians:

13 For you have heard of my former conduct in Judaism, how I persecuted the church of God beyond measure and tried to destroy it. 14 And I advanced in Judaism beyond many of my contemporaries in my own nation, being more exceedingly zealous for the traditions of my fathers.
Galatians 1:13-14 (NKJV)

All of these were Paul's gain before becoming a Christian. Yet as a Christian, these attributes no longer helped him. Even after his conversion on the Damascus Road, most of the Christians suspected it all was an act. Unfortunately, Christians cannot see inside a changed heart in the same manner God can. Instead of instantaneous acceptance, Paul had to prove himself. But with God's hand on Paul's life, and Paul's resolve in following the LORD, those actions were no longer a part of his walk. Perhaps no other New Testament Christian has received the abuse that Paul did, but he remained content, choosing to think of himself as the chief sinner in heaven (1 Timothy 1:15). Heavenly-mindedness helps us to overlook any inconvenience associated with the earth. That might be a debilitating disease, poverty, loneliness or a plethora of other difficulties. Most importantly, if we weigh our lives on a balance, we will realize that if we endure 100 years of pain on this earth it is still a great exchange for the price Jesus paid for our sins. Because of that great price, we will be in heaven for eternity. Paul's eyes had been trained to look back upon his own sin before reflecting upon his present condition. Shipwreck, beating, and pain could not begin to offset the joy he felt from his sins being forgiven, removed and forgotten by a God who loved him.

If involved in a trial, try Paul's approach. Remember your sin, counting it loss. Regardless of circumstance, be thankful for the amazing gifts God has given, including a future and a hope!

DISCUSSION QUESTIONS:

1. Do you spend more of your focus on your earthly retirement plan or your heavenly retirement plan? How do we store up treasures in heaven?

2. Talk about the person in your life who appears to best balance the difference between being in the world, but not being of the world. Are they happy?

3. King Hezekiah asked God for more years, and received what he asked for, but in that time, a son was born who caused much pain and sin in Israel. Have you endured any difficulty that you wanted to get behind you no matter what the cost? Prayer is an amazing gift, but should we be careful what we pray for?

4. Discuss the balance between caring about the morality of our world but not being overburdened by the social, economic and political realms. Is that balance possible?

5. God not only forgives our sin, but He forgets it, as well. Should we forget our sin, or remember it? Give an example of a benefit we can get by remembering our sin. Give an example of a benefit we can get by forgetting our sin.

Notes:

Notes:

Chapter 6,
Wasting Away with Worry!

Sometimes, we all need a little peace and quiet. Often, home is the best place for both. Yet there also are times when home becomes a place with too much extraneous input, whether it is due to the difficulty of turning off the television, the constant ringing of the telephone or the continuous presence of needy people. Before complaining, realize that at times, we are the needy ones in the lives of our friends or family members. That being said, man cannot supply our needs; only God can. God can and does use people to pass His blessings on to us, but He is the author and finisher of our faith.

¹ Therefore I exhort first of all that supplications, prayers, intercessions, and giving of thanks be made for all men, ² for kings and all who are in authority, that we may lead a quiet and peaceable life in all godliness and reverence. ³ For this is good and acceptable in the sight of God our Savior, ⁴ who desires all men to be saved and to come to the knowledge of the truth.
1 Timothy 2:1-4 (NKJV)

One of the secrets to that peace and quiet is prayer. Peace has been described as the absence of external disturbances while quiet is the absence of internal disturbances. When followers of the Lord have hearts of prayer, instead of worrying about the battles raging, those believers should hand the battles over to God. As David reminded King Saul and the Israelites when preparing to face the giant, Goliath, **the battle is the LORD's.** Because Jesus is the Commander in Chief of the LORD's army, we are mere foot soldiers. As foot soldiers, we are not required to make life-and-death decisions, but instead, our single choice is whether or not to follow Him. He does not push us into battle or sit on a hillside watching us fight. Instead, He leads us into battle, protects us in the battle and leads us home in victory.

In addition to describing how we can achieve God's gift of peace and quiet, Paul gives us a better understanding of the necessary types of prayer that will lead us there. First, in the verse quoted above from 1 Timothy, Paul mentions supplication, which comes from the Greek word *deesis*, (δέησις), meaning a wanting or a need. We all should comprehend what it is like to have needs, and the greatest need is for salvation. Through supplication, the Lord desires for us to pray for the needs of others, understanding that only God can supply the missing needs.

Secondly, Paul talks of "prayers," the Greek word *proseuche* (προσευχή). We are reminded of what prayer entails by James, the brother of Jesus:

Confess your trespasses to one another, and pray for one another, that you may be healed. The effective, fervent prayer of a righteous man avails much.
James 5:16 (NKJV)

As believers, we should pray fervently for our friends, for our families, for our neighbors and even for our enemies. According to James, our prayers can bring healing, and that healing may be physical, spiritual or both. Thirdly, we see that another aspect of our prayer life should be as intercessors. The Greek word for intercessory is the word *enteuxis (ἔντευξις)*, which is the word for "prayer" used in this verse:

¹ Now the Spirit expressly says that in latter times some will depart from the faith, giving heed to deceiving spirits and doctrines of demons, ² speaking lies in hypocrisy, having their own conscience seared with a hot iron, ³ forbidding to marry, and commanding to abstain from foods which God created to be received with thanksgiving by those who believe and know the truth. ⁴ For every creature of God is good, and nothing is to be refused if it is received with thanksgiving; ⁵ for it is sanctified by the word of God and <u>prayer</u>.
1 Timothy 4:1-5 (NKJV)

This word comes from a root meaning "to draw in closely or intimately." Technically, it is a term for approaching a king. We know that when Jesus died on the cross, the veil of the tabernacle was split, giving each believer access into the throne room of God. He is our King of kings, and we can draw in closely to Him anytime we want!

Let us therefore come boldly to the throne of grace, that we may obtain mercy and find grace to help in time of need.
Hebrews 4:16 (NKJV)

Though God is the Creator of all, He does not desire for us to approach Him as the Cowardly Lion approached the Wizard of Oz, nervously shaking and holding his tail. Instead, we are to come boldly to His throne, because He is a God of grace. Through grace, He has released us from the immense debt owed due to our sin. While Jesus offers intercessory prayer to the Father on our behalves (Hebrews 7:25), we are called to perform the same role for the lost! Reflecting upon our own lives, each of us should be able to remember what it was like before we had the knowledge of

91

grace. If surrounded by broken lives and broken people, we should have the understanding of the one step to mend the broken hearts and minds. Finally, Paul reminds us in 1 Timothy to be thankful for all men. It is easy to be thankful for people we think of as blessings, yet we are to be thankful for enemies, dishonest politicians and even the people who push our buttons. For God uses all things, positive and negative, to complete His work in us!

When a believer has an active prayer life, faith increases. Answered prayer reveals the Lord's intimate hand of guidance, as it reminds us that He is listening! When we learn to trust in His hand, we no longer waste precious time and energy in worry. Walking in that trust, we will find peace and quiet. Though we can have that peace and quiet in the noisiest situations, sometimes it is nice to get away to a place where birds are chirping, wind is blowing and raindrops are falling. It is then when it is easiest to be still and know that He is God (Psalm 46:10). Yet, even in the midst of turmoil, God can give us the peace that passes understanding. Though peace during turmoil might not make sense, it is certainly more of a miracle, pointing directly to God's hand!

If we really want peace and quiet, we should pray!

rather let it be the hidden person of the heart, with the incorruptible beauty of a gentle and quiet spirit, which is very precious in the sight of God.
1 Peter 3:4 (NKJV)

[11] that you also aspire to lead a quiet life, to mind your own business, and to work with your own hands, as we commanded you, [12] that you may walk properly toward those who are outside, and that you may lack nothing.
1 Thessalonians 4:11-12 (NKJV)

Worry points to lack of trust in the same way that covetousness points to lack of contentment. When we worry, we accuse God of lying, for He has promised that He will provide all of our needs. Without faith applying to our lives, our beliefs are only words! We should be content wherever He places us and trust Him, for He cares for us!

¹¹ Not that I speak in regard to need, for I have learned in whatever state I am, to be content: ¹² I know how to be abased, and I know how to abound. Everywhere and in all things I have learned both to be full and to be hungry, both to abound and to suffer need. ¹³ I can do all things through Christ who strengthens me.
Philippians 4:11-13 (NKJV)

This verse is often misquoted. Paul is stating that he has lived with much, and has also had little. With the help of Christ, we can be content in any circumstance.

"It isn't the mountain ahead that wears you out; it is the grain of sand in your shoe." Certainly, we can waste time worrying about those future mountains, but a minor inconvenience in the present is far more debilitating than a major hurdle yet to occur. That being said, the minor inconvenience in the present moves to the past so quickly! Typically, we find that our greatest worries rarely come to fruition. With that in mind, worry becomes one of the greatest time wasters in life, especially in the life of a believer.

Jesus had more to worry about than anyone else. He knew that those He came to save did not believe. He knew the Jewish leadership wanted to kill Him, and also knew that desire would become reality very shortly. Jesus knew that His impending death would be painful, humiliating and would create separation between Jesus and His Father. With the greatest right to worry, He still chose not to! Though we tend to think of "The LORD's Prayer" as the one that begins with, "Our Father, who art in heaven," if we really want to get insight into the prayer life of Jesus we should look at John 17. Just before enduring the cross, where He would carry each of our sins, Jesus prayed. In John 17:1-5, He prayed for Himself. Then in John 17:6-19, He prayed for His disciples. Finally, in John 17:20-26, Jesus prayed for each of us who would become His followers! Let's look at those verses, specifically about us:

[20] "I do not pray for these alone, but also for those who will believe in Me through their word; [21] that they all may be one, as You, Father, are in Me, and I in You; that they also may be one in Us, that the world may believe that You sent Me. [22] And the glory which You gave Me I have given them, that they may be one just as We are one: [23] I in them, and You in Me; that they may be made perfect in one, and that the world may know that You have sent Me, and have loved them as You have loved Me.
[24] "Father, I desire that they also whom You gave Me may be with Me where I am, that they may behold My glory which You have given Me; for You loved Me before the foundation of the world. [25] O righteous Father! The world has not known You, but I have known You; and these have known that You sent Me. [26] And I have declared to them Your name, and will declare it, that the love with which You loved Me may be in them, and I in them."
John 17:20-26 (NKJV)

In verse 23, Jesus explicitly mentions that the Father loves the world in the same way that He has loved Jesus. What a sweet prayer! None of us ever will endure any difficulty like the cross, but our prayer lives often can sound like broken records, asking for increased finances, better health or for trials to end. Instead, we should be praying for others, the special souls God has joined us with in this life. With all of the people who ever have been born throughout history, God could have placed us with any family, and could have had our lives intersect with any other lives. None of those lives that touch our lives are there by accident. We should respond with prayer! Answered prayer builds our faith, as it reminds us that God is not only listening, but that He cares. Most importantly, prayer changes us! We already know that we must endure tribulation, but through prayer, we can have His peace in the midst!

Jesus reminded us:

These things I have spoken to you, that in Me you may have peace. In the world you will have tribulation; but be of good cheer, I have overcome the world."
John 16:33 (NKJV)

Surely, we understand that a broken world filled with unbelievers will not be the most hospitable host to those choosing to follow God and God's Word! The greatest step is to take our eyes away from that world and focus on our future hope. Even in the midst of adversity in our lives, God still reigns on His throne of glory. Just because we will face tribulation does not mean that we walk that path without God's help or His care! A God who loves us immensely is not blind to a grain of sand in our shoes. Nor is that grain so small that it does not matter to Him! God already has promised us that as believers, He is going to complete His work in us...and we will overcome all difficulties!

[4] For whatever is born of God overcomes the world. And this is the victory that has overcome the world— our faith. [5] Who is he who overcomes the world, but he who believes that Jesus is the Son of God?
1 John 5:4-5 (NKJV)

Sir Edmund Hillary, the first man to summit the world's highest peak, Mt. Everest, said, "It's not the mountain we conquer, but ourselves." Jesus conquered the world for us. If His death on the cross was the end of the story, we would be in deep trouble. But because Jesus conquered death, and has asked us to join Him in that resurrection, we do not have a mountain to conquer. The victory lies in trusting God, who never will let go of us!

Be anxious for nothing, but in everything by prayer and supplication, with thanksgiving, let your requests be made known to God;
Philippians 4:6 (NKJV)

Most of us try to reinterpret that verse to say, "Be anxious for big issues, but try to handle the little ones on your own." But God wants us to trust Him. If we trust Him with the little issues, it becomes easier to trust Him in the big issues, too. We could spend a long time breaking down this verse in order to get a sufficient understanding. "Nothing" and "everything," both mentioned in this verse, are opposites. "Nothing" is a shortened version of "not one thing." Obviously, there is not **any** issues that should cause us to worry! At the same time, we should pray about every, single issue!

Some people do not want to bother God by praying about seemingly minor concerns. That is due to a misunderstanding of the character of God. He is not limited by time constraints. We may have 24 hours in each day, but God knows all (He is omniscient); He is everywhere at the same time (He is omnipresent); He has all power (He is omnipotent). That does not mean God has just enough power to manage! He can bring nuclear missiles to a marshmallow fight! Look closely at this verse:

[20] Now to Him who is able to do exceedingly abundantly above all that we ask or think, according to the power that works in us, [21] to Him be glory in the church by Christ Jesus to all generations, forever and ever. Amen.
Ephesians 3:20-21 (NKJV)

Paul, through the Holy Spirit, builds this verse perfectly. God can answer our prayers exceedingly. Not only that, He can answer those prayers exceedingly and abundantly! He can do that in all that we ask, but not only that, God has so much power, He can answer the prayers abundantly and exceedingly that we have not even prayed yet, even when we are still just thinking about praying! Spend some time looking at those adjectives:

exceedingly, abundantly, above all, above all that we ask, above all that we think, according to His power that works in us! Wow!

What do we have to worry about? :)

DISCUSSION QUESTIONS:

1. Two of the most important aspects of the Christian walk are prayer and Bible study. In prayer, we speak to God, and in Bible study, God speaks to us. This can be out of balance, when we only study the Bible and fail to pray, or if we only pray and fail to study the Bible. What are some of the signs in the life of a person who prays but does not study the Bible? Does this mean that person thinks their words are more important than God's words?
2. Similarly, what are some of the signs in the life of a person who studies the Bible but does not have an active prayer life? Remember, a big part of our prayer life should be concerning others! It seems like when our prayer lives and Bible study are out of balance it points to pride! Discuss this!
3. What has been the biggest worry of your life? Were you a Christian when this worry occurred? Discuss some of the times when God's answer to prayer in your life far outweighed the worry.
4. Discuss Bible characters and issues they worried about. Here is a list of a few if you have trouble finding someone: King Saul, King David, King Nebuchadnezzar, Nicodemus, the rich young ruler of Luke 18.
5. Discuss the similarities and differences between worry and fear.

Notes:

Chapter 7,
Standing on the Promises
of God

Faith has been described by many as blind, but in reality, faith just uses a different pair of eyes. Instead of "seeing is believing," we should understand that "believing is seeing." Belief opens our spiritual eyes! In Romans, Paul writes of an invisible God who is visible through His attributes, His creation and even His miracles:

**[20] For since the creation of the world His invisible attributes are clearly seen, being understood by the things that are made, even His eternal power and Godhead, so that they are without excuse, [21] because, although they knew God, they did not glorify Him as God, nor were thankful, but became futile in their thoughts, and their foolish hearts were darkened.
Romans 1:20-21 (NKJV)**

Certainly, all Christians can endure those times when faith falters, and this is a prevalent attack from Satan. The deceitful one tells us that God cannot forgive our sin, as it has been too egregious.

He tells us that we are not redeemable. Sadly, there are moments when he plants the tiniest seed that God does not exist. Yet all it takes is a little self-reflection to see those times when God made His presence unquestionable in our lives to know that He is with us. In the wilderness, God led the children of Israel as a pillar of cloud by day and a pillar of fire by night. They could see His presence, and still, when Moses ascended Mt. Sinai, Aaron fashioned a golden idol from their jewelry. After six chapters about enduring trials, we should have reached a point of understanding how God stretches us in trials. The same trial that stumbled us earlier in our Christian walks should become easier to endure as mature Christians. For through trials, God strengthens us.

[2] Grace and peace be multiplied to you in the knowledge of God and of Jesus our Lord, [3] as His divine power has given to us all things that pertain to life and godliness, through the knowledge of Him who called us by glory and virtue, [4] by which have been given to us exceedingly great and precious promises, that through these you may be partakers of the divine nature, having escaped the corruption that is in the world through lust.
[5] But also for this very reason, giving all diligence, add to your faith virtue, to virtue knowledge, [6] to knowledge self-control, to self-control perseverance, to perseverance godliness, [7] to godliness brotherly kindness, and to brotherly kindness love. [8] For if these things are yours and abound, you will be neither barren nor unfruitful in the knowledge of our Lord Jesus Christ. [9] For he who lacks these things is shortsighted, even to blindness, and has forgotten that he was cleansed from his old sins.
2 Peter 1:2-9 (NKJV)

As Peter states above, God has given us **"exceedingly great and precious promises,"** and then explains part of the process of God's nurturing hand in the midst of trials. We go from faith, to knowledge, to self-control, to perseverance, to godliness, to brotherly kindness, to love. Love is His end goal for each of us, that we may know His love and in turn, will learn to share that godly, *agape* love with others. It all comes back to the first step where our faith is standing upon those great and precious promises of God. It is not difficult when our lives are easy, but becomes a lifeline when in the midst of a battle.

What would the Lord have us do in the midst of this trial? Faith is not tested when everything is coming up roses. God never makes mistakes, so any situation that we find ourselves in has been designed specifically for us. With so many people hurting, we should focus upon standing on the promises of God. R. Kelso Carter, who lived from 1849-1926, wrote the words and music to the great hymn, and those words surely spoke loudly to the folks enduring the Great Depression only a few years later.

"Standing on the promises of Christ my King, through eternal ages let his praises ring;
Glory in the highest, I will shout and sing, standing on the promises of God.
Standing on the promises that cannot fail, when the howling storms of doubt and fear assail, by the living Word of God I shall prevail, standing on the promises of God.
Standing on the promises of Christ the Lord, bound to Him eternally by love's strong cord, overcoming daily with the Spirit's sword, standing on the promises of God.
Standing on the promises I cannot fall, listening every moment to the Spirit's call, resting in my Savior as my all in all, standing on the promises of God.
Standing, standing, standing on the promises of Christ my Savior; standing, standing, I'm standing on the promises of God."

What a great reminder! God's Word is filled with His promises to us, and He has not broken a promise. That is the beauty of His Word, as we can see time and time again, how steadfast He is to

101

follow through on every promise. Sometimes, when we are going through tough times, it is better to remind ourselves of these promises, rather than to struggle in the trial. In the remainder of this chapter, we will discuss six of those promises, though understand that the Bible is filled with promises to us:

1.   1 John 1:8-10
2.   1 Corinthians 10:13
3.   Romans 8:28
4.   1 Thessalonians 5:16-18
5.   Philippians 1:6
6.   John 14:3

Let's begin by cleaning up!

⁸ If we say that we have no sin, we deceive ourselves, and the truth is not in us. ⁹ If we confess our sins, He is faithful and just to forgive us our sins and to cleanse us from all unrighteousness. ¹⁰ If we say that we have not sinned, we make Him a liar, and His word is not in us.
1 John 1:8-10 (NKJV)

We cannot help but pick up some dirt in our daily walks, no matter how much we focus on God and the teachings of God. What can begin with the best attempt can turn into the worst in a matter of moments. Tell a child to "be good" and we have set him up for failure, as with sin nature, we cannot be good! "Act good, for a while," is much more manageable! We are children of God and in the same manner that a child cannot be good all of the time, we cannot either. We have moments of following the Lord, but God has reminded us that we are sinners, saved by His grace. But God is good, and He is faithful to forgive us when we come to Him.

Can we really make God a liar? No! He is incapable of telling a lie. What the passage is saying is that if we were telling the truth by saying that we have not sinned, God would be wrong. But we cannot last even one day without sinning. Simply by saying we are not sinners, we have sinned by lying! We are all sinners, and will continue to be sinners until we are united with our Savior. For those of us who have accepted Jesus into our hearts as Lord and Savior, He forgave every sin that we ever committed when we came to Him. He also forgave every sin that we ever will commit. This is not a license to sin, but God understands our nature of sin. The prophet, Jeremiah, reminds us that:

"The heart is deceitful above all things,
And desperately wicked;
Who can know it?"
Jeremiah 17:9 (NKJV)

When we come to the Lord, He replaces that heart of stone with a heart of flesh. As much as we love the Lord, we continue to sin, and it feels horrible to blow it over and over again, as if we are letting God down, but for Him to feel disappointment would mean that He had other expectations. Every sin that we commit, God knew we would commit! And still He saved us!

God reminds us that we are to confess our sins. If we do, He promises to forgive our sins and cleanse us from all unrighteousness. We have an awareness of some sins, but in regard to others, we walk in unawareness. If we confess the sins that we are aware of, He also will forgive and cleanse us from the sins we are unaware of! Often, he brings to remembrance sins that we need to confess.

Financial struggles often can lead us into a place where we question God. Yet God did not promise to supply all of our selfish desires. Instead, He promised to take care of our needs! What if we lose our jobs? What if we miss some meals? Does it really matter in the grand scheme of it all? In that grand scheme, believers in the Lord will spend all of eternity with Jesus, our Savior, who said:

[25] "Therefore I say to you, do not worry about your life, what you will eat or what you will drink; nor about your body, what you will put on. Is not life more than food and the body more than clothing? [26] Look at the birds of the air, for they neither sow nor reap nor gather into barns; yet your heavenly Father feeds them. Are you not of more value than they? [27] Which of you by worrying can add one cubit to his stature?

[28] "So why do you worry about clothing? Consider the lilies of the field, how they grow: they neither toil nor spin; [29] and yet I say to you that even Solomon in all his glory was not arrayed like one of these. [30] Now if God so clothes the grass of the field, which today is, and tomorrow is thrown into the oven, will He not much more clothe you, O you of little faith?

[31] "Therefore do not worry, saying, 'What shall we eat?' or 'What shall we drink?' or 'What shall we wear?' [32] For after all these things the Gentiles seek. For your heavenly Father knows that you need all these things. [33] But seek first the kingdom of God and His righteousness, and all these things shall be added to you.

[34] Therefore do not worry about tomorrow, for tomorrow will worry about its own things. Sufficient for the day is its own trouble.

Matthew 6:25-34 (NKJV)

With our physical sight focused on the things of this world, we tend to worry about food, clothing, our homes and our possessions. Yet our Savior had no place to lay His head when on this earth, often sleeping in the Garden of Gethsemane. Instead, we should focus upon our first step of cleanliness. God is willing and able to forgive us, but we need to confess. That freedom from sin is much more important than any difficulty on this earth. Remember Job's journey. His friends felt like Job's difficulties all came from sin. Job defended himself, but in doing so, fell into a place of self-righteousness that was sinful. As much as God loves us, we need to accept that any trial He places in our paths, He does for a reason.

Let us now proceed to the second promise.

God allows tests in each of our lives. In the first chapter of this book, we studied the similarity between a test and a trial, and the difference with the word temptation. Test and trials come from the LORD and temptation comes from Satan. This is easy to see with a little soul-searching, as God has no reason to desire for us to fall into sin. The word for trial in Greek is *peirasmo*, which is the state of being tested, often by suffering. Interestingly, it is the same word for temptation, which is a trial with a beneficial purpose. Even Jesus had to endure those trials and temptations when He walked as a man on this earth. Immediately after being baptized, Jesus fasted for 40 days and nights and then battled Satan's frontal assaults. Described by Matthew, Mark and Luke, we see that Satan offered Jesus the world. Jesus did not question Satan's ability to give the world to Jesus, as He knew that Satan had dominion over the earth. Yet Jesus remained sin-free and thwarted Satan with His knowledge of the Word of God. Satan misquoted or misinterpreted God's Word in all of his arguments to Jesus. This should remind us that while Satan is powerful, he is not ALL POWERFUL! He has spent thousands of years practicing his art of deceit. While he can pack quite a punch in his dealings with us as believers, he cannot battle the power of God. The power of God is available to us through the Bible, with God dwelling inside of every believer! How can we battle Satan without knowing what the Word says?

Sometimes trials and temptation can be intertwined. In a trial, God wants us to see His presence, where in temptation, Satan wants us to give in to sin. Sometimes, we endure a trial by relying on God and not giving in to temptation. This brings us to another powerful promise from our Lord:

No temptation has overtaken you except such as is common to man; but God is faithful, who will not allow you to be tempted beyond what you are able, but with the temptation will also

make the way of escape, that you may be able to bear it.
1 Corinthians 10:13 (NKJV)

Breaking this verse down, the first part is that we all stumble in the same ways. Second, we see that though we are not faithful, God is! Third, He only allows hurdles in our paths that we are able to jump over. When we find ourselves behind an approaching hurdle, God has a message for us. As difficult as the upcoming task may be, God is telling us that with His power, we have the strength that will sustain us. Jesus is the door and the way of escape. When we turn to Him, we are powered by God rather than powered by self. Remember, Satan brings the battle, but God allows that to happen for a purpose. Satan despises those who are working for the kingdom of God; certainly, the more we love the Lord, the bigger target will be on our heads from Satan. It may be difficult, but we should remember who is in charge of our lives! Through every trial, God is testing us, and just as silver is purified and made stronger under intense heat, God is drawing us closer.

This third promise is one of the greatest verses in the Bible. God has forgiven our sinful pasts and has promised us eternal lives for our futures. In between those two is the present, and there is no greater comfort than Paul's words in Romans:

And we know that all things work together for good to those who love God, to those who are the called according to His purpose.
Romans 8:28 (NKJV)

We often can feel conflicted, not knowing which direction to turn. GPS can help when driving, but there are times when even that technological advancement gets it entirely wrong. The Bible is our spiritual GPS, giving us the answers to many age-old questions. Yet some of those daily decisions do not seem to have a biblical answer. If we are being offered a job in New York City and another one in Tokyo, Japan, there is probably not a Bible verse that is going to tell us specifically which job to take! In cases like that, we are instructed to wait on the Lord, to pray, and to seek Him. When we do that, He often will open one door and close another. In biblical times, they cast lots, which would be the modern-day equivalent of rolling dice. God already knows which decision we will make!

Romans 8:28 is an amazing promise. It does not say that all things that we do correctly work out for our good, but all things. Every bad decision, God still can turn around for our good! What an amazing God! Just to make sure that we fall into this category, who are those who love God and are the called according to His purpose? Any who have asked Him into their hearts! When we are going through difficult times upon this earth, we sometimes forget how brief those difficulties will last. Even if our trial lasted for 70 years, it would pale in comparison to the amount of time we are going to spend with Him for eternity.

One way of grasping this is to understand the difference between God's perfect will and His permissive will. Think of a detour sign. While it may take less time to travel directly from point A to point B, when we choose a waypoint that sends us on a wild-goose chase, God faithfully brings us back to the path He has designed for us! Do we see the Lord in each of those detours? No, but He certainly is there, guiding our paths.

Your word is a lamp to my feet
And a light to my path.
Psalms 119:105 (NKJV)

Robert Frost wrote, "Two roads diverged in a wood, and I--I took the one less traveled by, and that has made all the difference." God's path is the one with all His blessings (not finances). That road more traveled by is the one with all the potholes, which cause us to trip and fall! If following the world, we are on the path to destruction.

¹³ "Enter by the narrow gate; for wide is the gate and broad is the way that leads to destruction, and there are many who go in by it. ¹⁴ Because narrow is the gate and difficult is the way which leads to life, and there are few who find it.
Matthew 7:13-14 (NKJV)

Yet there is a difference between the path and the gate. As Christians, we occasionally can find ourselves on the wrong path, but God will make sure He gets us to the right gate! So take another step and stand on this promise!

This fourth promise involves action, rather than just belief. Instead of worrying and complaining when difficulties arise, we should remember that God is still on the throne and also that He told us that this life would be a real challenge. This directly conflicts the message of the prosperity gospel. Having discussed some promises that give a believer power, we need to notice a promise that is noticeably absent. God has not promised that our Christian lives will be easy. Every one of the disciples of Jesus died as martyrs, except for John, and John was placed in a cauldron of burning oil! If God offered riches to everyone who turned to Him, would not everyone come for that reason alone?

Instead, Jesus told us:

¹⁸ "If the world hates you, you know that it hated Me before it hated you. ¹⁹ If you were of the world, the world would love its own. Yet because you are not of the world, but I chose you out of the world, therefore the world hates you. ²⁰ Remember the word that I said to you, 'A servant is not greater than his master.' If they persecuted Me, they will also persecute you. John 15:18-20 (NKJV)

Jesus also told us:

These things I have spoken to you, that in Me you may have

108

peace. In the world you will have tribulation; but be of good cheer, I have overcome the world."
John 16:33 (NKJV)

So, do not be surprised when life is difficult! When it is difficult, stand on His promises and follow this advice:

[16] Rejoice always, [17] pray without ceasing, [18] in everything give thanks; for this is the will of God in Christ Jesus for you.
1 Thessalonians 5:16-18 (NKJV)

This verse does not say to give thanks for all the seemingly wonderful things in our lives; it says to give thanks for everything. It is difficult to imagine a parent thanking God after the death of their child, but Job did exactly that. In fact, he thanked God for not just the death of one child, but for the death of all 10 of his children. God deserves our praise and our thanks. This relies heavily on the other promises God has made to believers. If we have accepted Him into our lives, and He has forgiven our sins, we do not need anything else! If we truly believe that all things will work together for our good, then even the death of a child, the loss of a job or the brokenness of our lives will be for our good. We just need to thank Him for it.

When looking around, it may seem as if we are in the darkest hole imaginable. Yet how dark can it be with Jesus Christ as our Lord and Savior? He is the Light of the world, and light cannot exist with darkness. That place might seem dark, but all we have to do is open our spiritual eyes and see the Light! Prayer is an incredible gift to each Christian, the ability at any moment to enter into the throne room of God and speak with Him! In prayer, God changes our hearts, and brings them in line with His heart. Instead of spending the majority of our prayer time asking for things, our prayers should concern the lives of others, whom God has placed beside us. But at the heart of each prayer should be thankfulness. Instead of praying for increase, we should be thanking God for His hand of provision and love.

In this fifth promise, the focus changes to the end of our lives.

³ I thank my God upon every remembrance of you, ⁴ always in every prayer of mine making request for you all with joy, ⁵ for your fellowship in the gospel from the first day until now, ⁶ being confident of this very thing, that He who has begun a good work in you will complete it until the day of Jesus Christ; Philippians 1:3-6 (NKJV)

Everyone walking this earth begins with an addiction to sin, and typically, even when trying to conquer sin, our failures occur when pride gets in the way. Just as Peter bragged to Jesus, "I love you more than the rest; I am willing to die for you," on the same night that he denied Jesus three times, we get in trouble by using sweeping generalizations like never and always. Modern-day culture seems to honor self-confidence, without understanding how often that self-confidence passes to pride. Interestingly, in all 14 times the word "confident" is used in the Bible, it is a positive attribute when relying upon God and is a negative attribute when relying upon self.

How can we be confident that we will conquer that sin addiction? Because God is going to complete His work in us! That has nothing to do with our own actions, as we are merely the recipients of His gift! Without our eyes focused upon our Gift-Giver, we are destined for failure.

"A proud man is always looking down on things and people; and, of course, as long as you're looking down, you can't see something that's above you." -- C.S. Lewis

When a man brags about his accomplishments, there always is exaggeration, if not hyperbole. By looking at any job seeker's resume, this prideful exaggeration is apparent. Instead of having

110

absolute confidence in our past, we should have confidence in God's future in us. Confidence in self is fleeting, yet confidence in God is perfect knowledge, irrefutable because of His promises!

We fail, but God never fails. He is the one responsible for us becoming more like Him. He will put us in situations where we will grow closer to Him. God is going to complete His work in us. So what is our part in this formula? This is very important. God is going to keep teaching us lessons, through the various trials of life. Before qualifying for the Olympics, the athletes have to prove themselves in the Olympic Trials. In the same manner, we endure trials to become more like the Lord.

² My brethren, count it all joy when you fall into various trials, ³ knowing that the testing of your faith produces patience. ⁴ But let patience have its perfect work, that you may be perfect and complete, lacking nothing.
James 1:2-4 (NKJV)

Lessons are not always easy. Sometimes, we have to get gently prodded in one direction. When we fail to listen, sometimes we have to get hit in the head! The shepherd's staff worked in both ways. The crook at the end could gently bring the straying sheep back. If the sheep went astray too many times, the shepherd might choose to pop the sheep in the butt with the staff to get the sheep's attention. If we learn the first time, we are more apt to get the gentle correction rather than the attention getter. We should learn our lessons well.

If God is going to perfect us, why did He not make us perfect the first time? Why did He allow us to live in these sinful bodies on this sinful earth? Paul certainly understood that feeling:

¹⁵ For what I am doing, I do not understand. For what I will to do, that I do not practice; but what I hate, that I do. ¹⁶ If, then, I do what I will not to do, I agree with the law that it is good.

111

¹⁷ But now, it is no longer I who do it, but sin that dwells in me. Romans 7:15-17 (NKJV)

Though we hate sin, we continue to sin! It is difficult to get puffed up with pride when we easily look into that mirror and see a sinner saved by God's grace. He has promised to never leave us or forsake us, and as our Teacher, to complete His work in us. One man stated that sixth grade was the most difficult three years of his life. God does not tell us the length of His instruction until we graduate, but He did tell us that we are going to graduate!

Finally, we get to the sixth promise:

The old phrase that "home is where you hang your hat" is certainly a truth in many ways. Though vacations are fun, it is always a blessing to go home, to sleep in the bed we are most accustomed to. Additionally, home is where all of our "stuff" is, the boxes and boxes of possessions that evoke memories of our lives. Yet it is interesting that when a fire, landslide or other disaster is drawing nigh, the objects that we desire the most are the photos of our dearest family and friends. "Things" can be replaced, but memories have to be created anew. Most of us have friends who recently have lost their homes, as the economy remains unstable. Additionally, the number of homeless people seems to be increasing. Though God has promised to supply our needs, Jesus was homeless. Regardless of whether or not we have a roof over our head, we have a home. It is with the Lord:

¹ "Let not your heart be troubled; you believe in God, believe also in Me. ² In My Father's house are many mansions; if it were not so, I would have told you. I go to prepare a place for you. ³ And if I go and prepare a place for you, I will come again and receive you to Myself; that where I am, there you may be also. ⁴ And where I go you know, and the way you know." John 14:1-4 (NKJV)

Many of God's promises involve this world, but this final promise involves our future. If God created the universe in six days, imagine how amazing our home in heaven will be, as Jesus has been preparing it for almost 2,000 years! On this earth, we put so much emphasis on our homes. They need to be just right for entertaining, as we do not want others to see the house in disarray. Yet the truth is, God can provide for us whether we are in a mansion, a studio apartment or on a bus bench! What is most important is that we all realize this is not our home! God is outside of the dimension of time, and according to Hebrews, sees us as seated in the heavens already. We are travelers on this earth, not residents, as our home is with God. Home is not really where we hang our hats. Home is where we hang our hearts!

Life's difficulties remind us of the unselfish prayer of Elijah. He prayed for a three-and-a-half-year drought to occur on the nation of Israel. That prayer was unselfish because the ensuing drought and famine would affect Elijah, too. Yet he was willing to endure the hardship so that others would be drawn to the Lord. All of us find the Lord in our brokenness. That is because of pride. When we finally realize that we cannot do it on our own, we turn to the only One who can do it for us, Jesus! We should be willing to endure hardship so that others will come to know Jesus Christ as their Lord and Savior.

Trials are real and often painful. But to endure those trials, we have a God who loves us who is willing to lead us through each step. Possibly the biggest hurdle is learning to trust Him. That trust is called faith, and in the best of times, it is only a word. When times get tough, faith must become an action verb. Four times in the Bible, we see the statement that, **"The just shall live by faith."** An actor delivering his lines can change the meaning of the sentence by choosing which word to emphasize. Sometimes, when he does not grasp the personality of the role he is playing, that emphasis can greatly alter the portrait that the director is attempting to paint. Often, that occurs when he takes one line out of context, as a deeper reading will offer a deeper understanding. Many times, directors instruct the actors how to deliver the line correctly, at least in their own interpretation of what they would like to see on the stage or screen.

In the Bible, there are many verses that are either quoted or repeated. Since the entire Bible is God-breathed, those repetitive verses are reminders to us that we should spend enough time reading to comprehend the meaning of those verses. When God speaks to us, if we do not listen, He tells us again. How many times do parents have to remind their children? Just because a child does not choose to acknowledge the parent's instruction does not mean that the parent simply surrenders by ceasing that instruction. Instead, most parents become more demonstrative with their words, as they pass the point from encouragement to demand.

One of those repetitive verses comes from a minor prophet in the Old Testament book of Habakkuk. The difference between Major Prophets and Minor Prophets has nothing to do with power. Instead, the Major Prophets are called that because their books are longer. Yet the Minor Prophets spoke with the same power, but packed that power into fewer words. Most of us should be familiar with the phrase in the fourth verse:

² Then the LORD answered me and said:
"Write the vision
And make it plain on tablets,
That he may run who reads it.
³For the vision is yet for an appointed time;
But at the end it will speak, and it will not lie.
Though it tarries, wait for it;
Because it will surely come,
It will not tarry.
⁴"Behold the proud,
His soul is not upright in him;

But the just shall live by his faith.
Habakkuk 2:2-4 (NKJV)

Three more times in the New Testament, this verse is quoted, yet each of those quotations seem to emphasize a different word.

¹⁶ For I am not ashamed of the gospel of Christ, for it is the power of God to salvation for everyone who believes, for the Jew first and also for the Greek. ¹⁷ For in it the righteousness of God is revealed from faith to faith; as it is written, "The just shall live by faith."
Romans 1:16-17 (NKJV)

In Romans, when quoting Habakkuk, Paul describes the process of how a sinner can come into the presence of a righteous God. It occurs through justification, which is the opposite of condemnation. In justification, God pardons those who believe in the work of Jesus Christ on the cross. To be justified is to walk in the knowledge that it was "just if I'd" never sinned! So in this passage, Paul emphasizes the word, "just," as in "the **just** shall live by faith!" This verse is quoted again in Hebrews:

³² But recall the former days in which, after you were illuminated, you endured a great struggle with sufferings: ³³ partly while you were made a spectacle both by reproaches and tribulations, and partly while you became companions of those who were so treated; ³⁴ for you had compassion on me in my chains, and joyfully accepted the plundering of your goods, knowing that you have a better and an enduring possession for yourselves in heaven. ³⁵ Therefore do not cast away your confidence, which has great reward. ³⁶ For you have need of endurance, so that after you have done the will of God, you may receive the promise:
³⁷"For yet a little while,
And He who is coming will come and will not tarry.
³⁸ Now the just shall live by faith;

But if anyone draws back,
My soul has no pleasure in him."
Hebrews 10:32-38 (NKJV)

In the passage above, we see the importance of endurance in our lives. Though God illuminates our lives with His presence, we continue to endure earthly difficulties and sufferings. He reminds us to confidently stay the course, regardless of those trials. Upon quoting Habakkuk, this time, emphasis is on the word, "live," as "the just shall **live** by faith!" Certainly, it is no surprise where Paul is going next:

¹⁰ For as many as are of the works of the law are under the curse; for it is written, "Cursed is everyone who does not continue in all things which are written in the book of the law, to do them." ¹¹ But that no one is justified by the law in the sight of God is evident, for "the just shall live by faith." ¹² Yet the law is not of faith, but "the man who does them shall live by them."
¹³ Christ has redeemed us from the curse of the law, having become a curse for us (for it is written, "Cursed is everyone who hangs on a tree"), ¹⁴ that the blessing of Abraham might come upon the Gentiles in Christ Jesus, that we might receive the promise of the Spirit through faith.
Galatians 3:10-14 (NKJV)

Lastly, in Galatians, Paul emphasizes "faith," as in "the just shall live by **faith!**" Faith is the hope of things not seen. As Christians, we understand that "believing is seeing," rather than the more often accepted statement that "seeing is believing." If we understand the power and principles of electricity, it is not blind faith to expect a light to go on when we turn the switch! Though we cannot see electricity, we have faith that the process will work. This is a wonderful example of the amazing depth that God offers each of us through His Word. This is such a simple phrase of only six words, "the just shall live by faith." With three of those words being emphasized in different New Testament passages, the statement changes meaning completely! Are we just, not by our own actions but by the saving grace of Jesus Christ? Are we willing to endure a life of trials for our Lord, with His promise of a heavenly life when this one is over? Are we willing to trust in Him with faith, standing on His promises regardless of the difficulties? God desires to hold our hands through it all. Trust Him. He loves us!

DISCUSSION QUESTIONS:

1. What promise that God makes in the Bible is your favorite? Why?

2. Does it take blind faith to believe in God, or does He reveal Himself to us in real and tangible ways that can make us certain of His existence?

3. More than just believing in the existence of God, what events have taken place in your life that reveal to you that God cares about all aspects of your life?

4. Though trials are difficult for all of us to endure, when we focus on the fact that God uses each trial to complete His work in us, it reminds us that He has a purpose and a plan. What are the steps we should take when we find ourselves in a trial? Should these steps change in different trials, or are the steps similar in each case?

5. Are there any trials you have had to repeat because you did not learn the intended lesson the first time around? If so, what was the trial? Did you approach the trial in a different manner the second time around? Do you think God places us in trials where we already have learned the lessons?

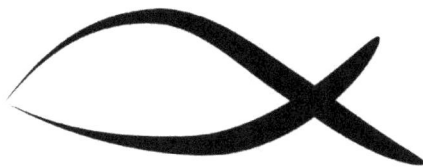

Notes:

Notes:

Notes:

Acknowledgments:

In 2011, I began this book, and trouble began to surround me. Financial hardship, health concerns and loneliness began to envelop me. God has a way of helping us to experience whatever we are teaching and writing about trials cast me into the fiery furnace. Sadly, instead of keeping my eyes focused on Jesus, I fell into a pit of despair and self-pity. Trust and faith in God turned to anger. Not only did I walk away from the project, but for five months, I turned my back on God. Even when we turn our backs on Him, He does not turn His back on us, though when I think about my illogical anger, it now seems like the dumbest time of my life. Most people want to ask, "How did that work out for you?"

For many of those months, I understood in my brain what was occurring, but could not convince my heart, as hard as I tried. Near the end of the year, one thought seemed to convince me. I realized that when I questioned God, I was calling Him a liar. Failing to trust Him included the same accusation. One weekend, I began working on this project again, hoping that getting back into the Word would bring my heart back to life. I spend 13 hours doing a word study on the difference between test, trial and temptation.

At the end of a long day, I was excited by some of the lessons in that study. When I attempted to save the 15 pages of notes and comments, my computer crashed! That laptop was the most expensive computer I ever had purchased, and it had lasted little over a year. The notes from that day, and the work from months before, was all gone. When it occurred, I knew that my cold heart had turned back to a heart of flesh again, as I began to pray, and praise the LORD for the computer crash. This time, it was not just words, but I began to trust Him again, that whatever occurs is in His plan!

Yet I did not feel strong enough to start the project again. Before it was completely gone from my brain, I wrote notes of what I learned that day. The biggest lesson was that God is not really testing us. He knows exactly what we are going to do in each circumstance. Instead, a trial is so we can see how God appears when we need Him! Trials increase our faith and help us to trust Him. In my trial that year, I did not trust God and turned away. Too bad for me, for most trials where we do not learn the intended lessons will have to be endured again.

In January of 2014, I once again focused my attention on this book on trials. Lo and behold, the trials began again. I cannot say that my faith never faltered, but I can say that this time, I stayed the course. I did not just write about how to endure trials. Instead, I endured trials, and as always, the LORD demonstrated His presence in the midst. On a side note, I will say that I am strongly considering joy as the subject for the next book, for I sure would like to experience that for an extended period of time!

To culminate this journey, I would like to acknowledge some people who continue to share the road I am on, and who keep my iron sharpened. God has placed three men in my life who give much more than encouragement, Jeff Kirst, Dave Rann and Todd Williams. Thanks again, my brothers from different mothers!

I also would like to acknowlege my small group Bible study. Tom Thorne and Anthony Herron keep coming to our Saturday morning studies where I teach each of these chapters as I write them. It is a great way of seeing typographical errors or in our discussions, find out if there are sections that need more explanation.

Thanks goes to my family, too. Gwen, Stacey and Julee each have their own trials to endure, but I am thankful that each one of them desires a relationship with God. Tracy and Joel are on the same journey. Trials for each of them might be the blessing of children, as I hope that I was a blessing, and not just a trial for my parents!

I am a deeply flawed man who is still so thankful for the LORD's forgiveness in my life. Someday, this journey of life will end, and with it, all of the sadness, trials, temptations and sin. What a day of rejoicing that will be, to bow down before my Savior. Until that time, I pray that I can stay busy in His work!

Blessings, my friends. Please feel free to share any comments with me through email.
gg4jesus@gmail.com

Garry Glaub

Other Media by Garry Glaub:

Strength & Beauty, the Book of Ruth
(2014)

To God Be the Glory Daily Devotional
(2011)

Throughout Your Generations, a Christian Seder
(2013)

"Here Am I! Send Me."
A Commentary on Isaiah 1-23
(2007)

Please feel free to watch my videos on YouTube under the name gg4jesus.

And check out my website:
www.garryglaub.com

www.ingramcontent.com/pod-product-compliance
Lightning Source LLC
Chambersburg PA
CBHW071005040426
42443CB00007B/675